You Glow, Girl!

RISE to Your Best Life and SHINE

Amanda,

Keep on glowing!

xo,

Beth Wilson-Parentice

Beth Wilson-Parentice

Contents

"And suddenly you know
it's time to start something new
and trust the magic of beginnings."

—Meister Eckhart

Introduction

LADIES—TODAY IS THE day I start the book that has been in the making for a long time.

There have been a few recent major life events that have inspired me to start writing. The biggest change is that I recently left a CEO role in my own company and I'm now also a single mom.

About a decade ago, I had an idea for an organic soda/cocktail mixer that I created in my own kitchen, which soon became my "Little Engine that Could," and grew it into a multimillion-dollar national beverage brand. When I launched my beverage company, I had no idea how big it would be—but I knew that if it did indeed become big, I wanted it to inspire others. Vapid corporate greed—not my thing. I wanted everyone, especially women, to know that if *I* could make this happen, then *they* could too. That was when I created the acronym for my brand Sipp: Strength, Inspiration, Passion, and Perseverance. This brand-ethos kept my flame burning every step of the way, knowing that I was forging a path for others to take them from "Impossible" to "I'm possible." And that's what this book is about: "the possible."

But as I transitioned from my CEO role, I felt the need to find a greater purpose—something bigger and more meaningful.

All along my journey; from childhood to Sipp to now, there have been ups and downs; and at each step—good, bad, and ugly—someone one would say, "that would make a great chapter in your book!" Each time I thought, *Who, me? Who would possibly want to hear about that?*

That, my friends, is the voice I call Negative Nancy; the champion of fear and self-doubt. Negative Nancy used to occupy an enormous space in my life. But as I began to search for greater meaning post-Sipp, as I became more intentional about sharing my life experiences to help others; Negative Nancy grew smaller.

Someone told me recently that the experiences I share with others is a gift and it is my duty to share it with the world.

This book is my gift to you and to the world. It is my hope that you or someone you know will gain strength and clarity from my experiences (and maybe you'll be able to silence your own Negative Nancy as well!).

Within these pages I will share my authentic self, how I never thought I could *ever* grow a beverage brand without beverage experience and uh, also be a mom and deal with challenges in my marriage that not a soul in the world knew about. There were times when I felt isolated and alone, but I knew I needed to step up and reach outside my comfort zone. I needed to do something bold despite my feelings of self-doubt and my frenemy Negative Nancy. The challenges I faced knocked me down and they could have kept me down. But I tackled one obstacle at a time and as I managed to turn each one around, I built up my confidence slowly but surely and began to face my fears head on.

Everyone is born with a light burning inside of them, but all the outside influences from childhood onwards start to dampen our flame. Were you a child of divorce, abuse, neglect, or bullying? Imagine what that did to your flame. And now as an adult what challenges are threatening to snuff out your flame like a gust of wind—job loss, death, bad marriage, infertility, sickness?

Now is the time to reignite that flame. It might be dim from time to time, but it's your job to keep it glowing brightly for all the world to see—and I'm here to help.

You are the only you—one-of-a-kind. Dismiss the negativity and keep your flame glowing brightly.

I welcome you to join me on a journey as I share how I discovered that the more I stepped outside my comfort zone and took chances, the more I learned about myself, which caused life-changing experiences to happen. There were many times my flame almost went out, but I refused to let anyone dim my light.

Over time, those experiences encouraged me to *finally* open the door, dream big, and unleash my inner sparkle; with passion, perseverance, and courage. I hope my stories empower and inspire you to do the same; and to be the best version of yourself!

If I can do it, you can too (in your own way) and I will be there along for the ride to make sure that *you glow, girl*!

Red

"Can you remember who you were, before the world told you who you should be?"

—*Danielle LaPorte*

THIS QUOTE HAS always stuck with me. Who was that little girl before all the outside forces started telling me? I was creative, shy, and wanted to fly with paper wings I skillfully crafted. Despite being introverted, I had BIG plans. I planned to carry my dad's larger-than-life ladder from the garage to the back of our ranch house, climb to the roof, attach the wings to my arms and jump while flapping my little arms as fast as they could go.

I dreamt night after night about the amazing things I would see once I finished my wings and took flight. I still remember that feeling of pure joy and wonderment. Luckily, for my own safety, I couldn't manage to even get the big ladder down off the wall, much less move it out to the roof, so I had to resort to the next highest flight platform…the picnic table! I jumped and flapped as hard as I could and when I plummeted straight to the ground; I went right back to the drawing board planning new and improved wing concepts.

By now you're probably asking: "What does this have to do with the chapter name, Red?" Well, I'm getting to that. Red is an incredibly meaningful word to me. I have red hair and "red" was how I was identified in elementary school. Well, actually there were other names too, like Fireball and Carrot Top. Imagine this: I'm walking around school trying to feel all good about myself with my new shiny shoes, my favorite purple jeans and cool-girl backpack and I hear, "Hey, Red!" and then a bunch of kids' laughter comes echoing down the hall.

Am I a freak? I thought. *Why me? Why do I have this strange bright red hair and freckles?*

Instead of embracing my uniqueness, it was one of those defining moments that lingers into adulthood and needs to be kicked to the curb. When thoughts like "am I a freak" began to appear was when my dream of taking flight with custom handmade wings started to disappear.

What memory do you have before the world told you who you should be? Bring yourself back there. Feel those feelings— let them wash over you. Shut out all the noise. We *need* to go back and remember.

Whenever I start thinking that I can't do something, I think, *why can't I? Who's really telling me that I can't do it?*

Do you ever hear that voice in your head saying, "why waste your time on that—you can't do it, that's stupid, what are you thinking?!" Name that voice and when you hear it again, call it by name (feel free to use Nancy!). Politely ask her to sit down and be quiet (or shut up!). Then immediately bounce that negative with a positive. Flip the script.

For example, if Negative Nancy ever starts to whisper, "My book will never be a bestseller, so why bother?" then I counter with "If I finish my book and help just one person, then it will be a huge accomplishment!". And I not only think this positive thought, I say it out loud, too.

Now it's your turn. Listen to what your critic is saying, then counter it with a positive antidote. Say it out loud. Rinse and repeat! Doing this will ultimately allow you to shift your mindset.

When I felt the calling to write this book, I was in a full-on battle with Nancy! She showed up more than usual. The more I pushed forward, ignoring her voice, she showed up less and less. The more you push past your internal critic, you dilute their power and amplify yours.

This is your life. *You* make the decisions. Don't let that negative voice tell you what you can and can't do. "It" can't control you. Take it along for the ride and show it what you can do. Prove it wrong. Only you have the power to create the life you desire, and the truth is if you don't go after what you want, you'll never get it.

I was extremely shy as a child and after my parents' divorce at age seven, I became even more withdrawn. We moved out of my childhood home and I moved into an apartment with my mom in an unfamiliar town. I had to go to a new school. I saw my dad every weekend, but it was a huge adjustment. My mom was working full-time, and I had to walk home from school on a busy street and go to a neighbor's house until she picked me up after work. I felt alone and faked being sick over twenty times that year so that my mom would stay home with me. That was until she found my journal that basically read as a full-on confession. What was I thinking putting it in writing? She obviously was not happy to make this discovery and told me that she was going to lose her job if I kept it up. Of course, I felt guilty. This was a scary time for me, and that bright flame I had went down to the tiniest flicker.

A child is pure and glows with a bright flame. A child does not deserve to be neglected, shamed, or abused. You didn't deserve the things that might have happened to you. You were an innocent *child*, for God's sake! Why is it we feel responsible for so many things when we were only a child? And then make ourselves pay the price for it, forever.

I remember when I was around nine-years-old my mom was dating someone. I guess it was pretty serious, because after a while she told me that she was considering marrying him, and she wanted to know my thoughts. Do you know what I based my opinion on? The fact that he took me out to Friendly's (the ultimate ice cream diner on the east coast of the U.S.) every Thursday night when she was in night school and bought me my favorite hot fudge sundae. I know, crazy right? She decided to marry him, and it turned out that the fun "friendly" guy I saw every Thursday night was actually a narcissistic, demanding, mean, abusive man. Needless to say, the marriage ultimately ended and how do you think I felt? *How could I have been so stupid? How could I have not seen who he was?* The answer should have been, how *could* I have seen who he really was? I was nine! But still, I thought it was my fault.

Have you ever thought about why you can't move forward or are so self-critical?

Sometimes we masterfully avoid the pain by ignoring that inner child and if left unattended, she dictates how we make decisions, react to challenges, and has an outside influence on how we live our life—and we may be none the wiser.

Think about a time when as a child you made a "bad" decision, or you felt like something "happened" because of you. Take a moment and forgive yourself. Tell yourself *out loud*, it's not your fault. Tell your inner child she is now loved and appreciated by you and has nothing to feel guilty or ashamed about. None of what happened to her was ever her fault. She was just a child and had no way to escape—but now she is free! Make sure your inner-child knows you will be her champion from now on. You will be her protector, so be sure to let her know how proud you are of who she has become.

Only *we* can heal the pain of our inner-child. Trust me, I know because for years I thought someone else could do that.

One of the quickest ways we can destroy ourselves is to hold on to shame and regret. To move forward, we need to learn from our past mistakes and accept ourselves for who we truly are. Understand that everything that's transpired on our journey of life has made us who we are today.

For as long as I can remember I wanted to be an artist. I loved to draw. It was my passion. In my elementary school scrapbook, there was a page for each year that asked, "What do you want to be when you grow up?" Every year, I filled in the blank with "artist." There was never a doubt in my mind. I had the "crazy" idea that when I grew up, I would paint with an easel on the streets of Paris while wearing a little beret. I guess I wasn't concerned about how I would make a living!

I took my drawing pad everywhere. I think being an only child, my pad was like a sibling to me. When I had to go places where there were only adults, I had my pad and I drew. I drew so much that I won drawing contests and awards. My drawing enabled me to keep my flame glowing through some dark times. And drawing funny comic strips helped too!

When I entered high-school, I was so excited for art class. This was the big time now and I felt like I was on my way to being famous. Except things didn't quite turn out as I had planned. While I was in a top school district, there was only one art teacher who had been there for at least 100 years; or so it seemed. There was nothing inspiring about her. No spark, no glow. I think her flame went out years earlier, and she was miserable in her life and just going through the motions until she could retire.

Then here I come, all of fourteen, bright-eyed and bushy-tailed ready to learn and grow and be inspired. I think the brightness of my flame irritated her. Our class drawing projects never evoked any excitement. I tried my best, but she was always critical of my work. I thought that maybe she was just trying to push me harder, but when I saw her with other students, I thought possibly she just didn't have anything nice to say. She just generally seemed bothered my existence.

I worked harder and harder to prove myself and when I finally got the courage to tell her in my junior year that I wanted to be an artist; she chuckled in a cruel and dismissive way. I will never forget that moment and how it made me feel for as long as I live. That day changed the course of my life. The flame that I worked so hard to keep shining bright almost went out. I slowly stopped drawing, little by little, and when it was time to apply for college, my inner voice (damn you Negative Nancy!) said, "You'll never make it as an artist." So, I decided to major in business, because it would be the safer option for me.

Letting the criticisms of others affect us is bound to happen but letting it in our head (and letting it tear us down) will only stop us from doing something amazing. It will prevent us from sharing our gifts with others. My art teacher was supposed to be a mentor. She was the expert, or so I told myself. I listened to her, and eventually her negative comments fed Negative Nancy, and my glow got dimmer and dimmer. I allowed her to tell me how good I was. I gave up on something because I didn't think I would do as well as *she* thought I should.

I didn't know who I was then. I only knew who I wasn't.

Now, as an adult, I tell my inner child that my art teacher was human, just like all of us. She may have had broken dreams herself. I won't allow her negative comments and dismissiveness to dim my glow any longer. I'm proud of my artistic gift, and I am so fortunate to have opportunities to design and create in my businesses. That experience was one of many that brought me to where I am today. I was bitter about it in the past, but now I'm grateful for it because I believe this is where I'm supposed to be.

I love these moving words from writer Erin Van Vuren: "Do you remember the child you once were? Do you remember the feeling of home in your belly as you laid down to drift into sweet sleep? There were no real stresses in those moments between you and the moon. That home is still inside of you. Buried beneath all the monsters that growing up brings. But monsters are only fears, you know. And children have a way of defeating them with light. Go find that child. Go find that home. Go find that light."

By embracing who we are, we can strip our negative inner voice of its destructive power and eventually our positive voice becomes louder, and our glow becomes brighter. Create a beautiful place inside yourself, and then expand outward and unleash your inner sparkle, girl!

A few of my favorite tips to transform negative experiences and thoughts into positive love for yourself…

1. Value your mistakes. Don't think of everything negative that has happened to you as something that wasn't supposed to happen to you. Perhaps it happened to get you to where you want to go. Grow through your negative experiences and find the positive on the other side.

2. What are the negative statements you tell yourself? Write them down. Then create positive statements to counter to your negatives. Practice saying them by changing the negative to a positive: "I let people walk all over me" becomes "I'm a giving person." "I'm so fat" becomes "I worked out two times this week because I'm committed to self-care."

3. Write positive affirmations on colorful sticky notes and put them around your house so if a negative thought creeps in, you have a positive affirmation right in front of you.

Glow Girl Affirmation:
I approve of myself and
love myself deeply.

2

Why Me?

"Women are so unforgiving of themselves. We don't recognize our own beauty because we're too busy comparing ourselves to other people."

—*Kelly Osbourne*

HY ME? Do you ever find yourself asking that? Do you ever have an answer?

Like any self-defense mechanism, asking "why me" can ease the pain and make us feel protected when things don't seem to be going our way. However, the truth is, it causes more damage because we end up feeling sorry for ourselves and resenting people for being "luckier" than us.

When bad things happen to us or we don't have the life we want, it's so easy for us to blame others. But the reality is, life is life and we *all* have the good and the bad. If you believe that everything that happens in your life is "done to you," you've given away your power.

Now when I ask myself "why me" the answer is, "why not me?" This is one of my favorite statements. I say this when I start to go down the path of comparing why bad things seem to happen to me, but others seem to have it all.

Try accepting reality rather than fighting it. If you wonder why you don't have a perfect life like other people, you are sabotaging yourself. You need to choose a different mindset.

When you stop expecting, you start accepting. And while we're spending time wondering 'why can't I be that person who has it all going on' or "why do only these bad things happen to me', we lose time we could be investing in ourselves, believing in ourselves, and ultimately not working towards making our dreams a reality.

I spent so much time looking at what other people had, and what I didn't. Where they were in life and I wasn't. It distracted me from focusing on me and my accomplishments.

After my son was born, it was hard for me to go out anywhere. He cried all the time. There were times when I just couldn't take the crying anymore and I would put him in his crib, turn the lullaby music on and close the door. I would go in our bedroom, turn the television on and wait ten minutes, while I cried. I felt like a terrible mother. When I could finally get him to sleep, I would attempt to take a shower, maybe for the first time in a week, and pray that when I turned the water off, he would still be sleeping. I would shower as quick as I could, count to ten, say a prayer and turn the water off. And... screaming baby!

I would rarely go out with him because of the crying. People would stare at me as I was trying to console him. They almost seemed to be trying to figure out if I was hurting him. I felt like the biggest failure and the worst mother in the world. Eventually, I tried to tell myself not be afraid to go out with him. I thought, *who cares what people think of me. They have no idea what I'm going through. Screw them.*

One brave day, I decided to listen to myself and headed to the farmers market that normally I would never dare do to because it was more than five minutes from my house. My husband had been gone for two days and he was coming home that night and I wanted to try to plan a romantic late-night diner with candlelight. I'd found a CD with white noise sounds that was guaranteed to get my baby to sleep within fifteen minutes at night (that's what the CD said!) and keep him asleep for at least two to three hours.

So, I ventured out on the quest of having an evening of romance with my husband and a sleeping baby. But even going to the farmers market was an experience. I'd planned to go in and get two Black Angus steaks, some fresh vegetables and maybe a dessert if I was lucky. I was on a colicky baby mommy mission. I had my list and literally ran through the market, giving my baby as much motion as possible in his stroller while perusing all the goodies. I did it in record time and was home free with only a few small cries…until I decided to treat myself to a café mocha. Why quit now? I thought. Maybe I could squeeze out another couple of minutes at the coffee bar booth. I was in line and only two people were ahead of me. So far, so good.

A woman stood in front of me in line with a double stroller. Oh God, I wondered, how does she do it? She smiled at me and I smiled back. I looked at her admiringly and said, "Wow, twins. They are so adorable." So, by now my time was expiring and my baby was starting to get fidgety because we weren't moving, and the whimpers were beginning to turn into wails.

I started to frantically push the stroller back and forth like an insane woman while chanting with my inside voice, "please don't cry, please for the LOVE OF GOD don't cry!" while my outside voice said, "They must be a handful," imagining my son times two.

Now I was breaking out in a sweat and I could feel heat, red hot heat, slowly enveloping my face. But did I stop, no. I continued, "Do you get much sleep?" I was now not only pushing the stroller back and forth to calm my "demon" child, but I managed to find a new side-to-side technique. The crying escalates.

She replies, "actually, they have been fabulous," beaming with pride and practically shouting to be heard over my screaming baby. No wonder she looked so put together and so rested. And to top it off, her babies were wearing perfectly coordinating outfits.

She then continues to say, "They've been sleeping through the night and they have this amazing bond." WTF! I was two seconds from about going gangsta-momma on her! I didn't want to hear this.

Oh, but hold on, it gets worse. She steps up to the barista and orders a low-fat cappuccino, *unsweetened.* Seriously? I thought, no wonder she looks good: she has amazing babies and drinks low-fat drinks, oh and I'm sure she eats organic food and does yoga.

We said our goodbyes, with a big (fake) grin on my face, she picked up her skinny drink and strolled away with her perfect smiling babies, her size two Gap pants and hip Nike slip-on sneakers.

She has it all, I thought. I couldn't understand why everyone else around me was blessed with such perfect, lovable babies and the perfect life. Even my friend, who wasn't expecting to have another child, was given an angel. She started sleeping through the night shortly after she was born and when she cried you could barely even hear it! One time she was crying, and I actually thought it was a cute little bird chirping. And she *always* looked happy. I could hold her for hours and barely hear a peep. When I would bring my son over her house, usually in a sleep deprived state of mind, I thought maybe some of her happy-go-lucky disposition would rub off on him. No such luck.

Everywhere I turned seemed to add fuel to the fire. Friends, strangers, the internet, moms groups. What the hell else was left?

As I was wallowing in my self-pity comparing myself to every mother I met, researching online what other moms of incessantly crying babies were doing, my mom suggested going to a weekend personal development seminar. I thought, how could I leave my baby? Who would have the patience to care for him? She offered to take care of him so I could go, saying how much it would help me. Honestly, I was so burnt out I couldn't even think about trying to retain anything that was going to personally develop me!

I dragged myself to the city, sleep-deprived to see what this was all about. For starters, they encouraged people to go up on stage and share their stories. *Hell no*, I thought. They should be lucky I'm even sitting in this chair with my eyes open and my hair brushed. They asked for a volunteer to come up and a woman was soon making her way toward the podium. I thought, *good luck girl. Have fun baring your soul to hundreds of strangers. Better you than me.*

As the woman got closer to the podium, I was thinking she looked familiar. I felt like I had seen her somewhere before. She introduced herself and started to tell her story. She began speaking with a very shaky voice while trying to keep the microphone close to her mouth and said, "Um...hi, um...I was married five years ago to a man I met on a blind date. He was wonderful and we had a great marriage." I thought, well this doesn't sound so bad. Then she paused and closed her eyes and I had a feeling this was about to take a turn for the worse. "We decided to start a family and were blessed with twins, a boy and a girl. We were so thrilled. They mean everything to me." Her voice started to crackle, and tears were streaming down her face now.

She took a deep breath and continued, "Two months ago I found out my husband was cheating on me with this girl at work. I was devastated, I mean my world just crashed...but told him I would try to work it out for the sake of the twins. Unfortunately, he didn't take me up on my offer." She sobbed, "He decided that he wanted to be with his twenty-year-old secretary and asked me for a divorce."

As if a lightning bolt had struck me, I remembered the woman. She was the woman with the perfect "twins" I had met at the farmers market. She said she was devastated, and she didn't know how she was going to take care of twins all by herself. She continued saying he was the love of her life. And the worst part was, he was getting married the next month and her husband and new girlfriend were now starting to fight for custody. She was weeping openly saying she just didn't know how to go on.

Oh my God. The woman I *thought* had it all was losing everything. Things are not always as they seem. I'd thought everyone had it better than I did, but that wasn't the case. I had a husband, a healthy child—even if he was difficult at times—and family and friends. And now I had an epiphany.

I was comparing myself and my life to something I *completely* imagined. Another person's life is never as perfect as your mind makes it out to be. When we compare, we end up only seeing the good in others and forget the good in ourselves. And we typically compare the worst of what we know about ourselves to the best assumptions that we make about others.

This was a huge wake-up call for me. This one impactful moment made me realize how much comparison had become a part of my life. Why is it we do something that makes us feel bad? Comparison is dishonoring our beautiful uniqueness and each time I compared, I dimmed my glow. I always told myself I would never let *anyone* dim my glow, so why was I allowing *myself* to do it?

Can you think of a time you've done this? How did it make you feel?

It's one of those crazy things that when you're doing it, you think it makes you feel better because it's allowing you to wallow in self-pity. These toxic comparisons blind us from seeing our strengths. Because somewhere between thinking, "I'll never be a mom like her" and "I'll never find a man who loves me like he loves her," we are stuck in self-pity and we forget how strong we are on our own.

And then once you lose your strength, it's impossible to see that there's another woman out there comparing themselves to *you* and feeling the same exact way.

I love this quote from fashion designer Diane Von Furstenberg: "You know there's a thing about the woman across the room. You see the woman across the room. You think. She's so poised; she's so together. But she looks at you and you are the woman across the room for her."

When comparison is used to find fault in yourself, it can be toxic. I call it, comparisionitis.

Seems like everyone is posting how wonderful their lives are, but we know social media never shows the full picture. They give us a snapshot and we fill in the blanks of the rest of their story, and create a life that we are envious of, without knowing the whole truth.

So many moms admit they are insecure (but truly aren't we ALL, sister?) and compare themselves to other moms and then end up feeling like failures. Especially new moms. I have a mom request. Let's strive to admire other moms and recognize how wonderful they are at what they do, without feeling like we are terrible failing moms. Love your children and do the best you can do and know that's enough.

The mind loves comparison and social media is its playground.

Checking your newsfeed or updating your status multiple times a day is not a helpful way to focus your energy. When you scroll through the news people are positing, how do you feel afterwards? While some posts can sometimes be helpful, it's difficult to not have feelings of envy when you see others having the time of their lives, especially when we may be suffering.

We see one moment and we fill in the blanks of the rest of their story, and create a life that we are envious of, without knowing the whole truth. Just remember, people don't post their "real" life, they post their "ideal" life. How can we ever compete with that?

Do you post and use social media to make yourself feel better? Some people aren't all they post to be and that's a slippery slope. If you are doing that now, stop. It has a way of backfiring. By posting how amazingly wonderful your life is, the façade could actually make you feel worse because now you're not living up to your *own* posts.

I realized the impact this was having on my life and my self-esteem. After my twin mom epiphany, I realized I needed to make a change. I needed to change my mindset. I started to only focus on myself and where I wanted to go on my journey.

Become your own standard. Learn to appreciate yourself for who you are, not for what you possess or your achievements.

Emulate, don't envy. If there is someone who inspires you, instead of thinking that you'll never have what they have, create a plan to replicate their success.

While we live in a comparison culture, we are all human and had to start somewhere. Don't compare your beginning to someone's middle or end. We tend to compare our behind-the-scenes with someone else's big moment. All we can see is their success, not the thousands of hours they've dedicated preparing and working toward their goal. Instead of letting other people's accomplishments allow you to be hard on yourself, let it be a catalyst for all you can be in life.

I was so hard on myself, but this experience helped to change my mindset. And that change helped me immensely as I was building my beverage business. There are so many beverages out there which makes it so easy to compare and think you can't ever get to where they are. I could have chosen to let that stop me so many times, but I chose to focus only on me and where I wanted to go.

Compare yourself to who you were yesterday. Focus on *your* accomplishments.

If you think you're behind, because you see someone further along, just remember, you are exactly where you're supposed to be. You're on *your* uncharted path and it's up to you to lay the stones to lead you to *your* destination. Just as we are incomparable, our journey is incomparable.

In reflecting back on my experience with my son, I asked "why me" so many times. Why was I given this baby who cried almost all his waking hours? When I answer, "why not me," it became clear that God gave him to me because I could handle it. I didn't see that then, but I didn't have confidence in myself or give myself credit that while it was incredibly challenging, I got through it one day at a time and my confidence grew every step of the way.

Be yourself and believe in yourself. A flower does not compete to the flower next to it—it just blooms! You are unique, you are special, you are beyond comparison so stop comparing your life and get glowing. Shine and let others shine too. We only get one shot. Focus on *you* and enjoy the crazy beautiful journey of *your* life!

A few of my favorite tips to combat comparisionitis...

1. Is there someone you admire? Do you have a role model? Instead of wishing you were like someone, find inspiration and learn from them. You can use it to identify goals you'd like to achieve. Work on the things you want change and at the same time know your self-worth and understand how unique you are. Remember, compare to learn only, not envy.

2. What negative reel do you play in your head when you see someone who you think has it better than you? Turn it off and honor yourself. Think about all

the things you DO have, the people you love and who love you, the blessings that life has given you. Practice gratitude for those you compare yourself to, celebrate their accomplishments and wish them well!

3. Take a digital detox! Use a timer alarm to limit the time you spend reading other people's posts on social media and don't go on after a certain time in the evening. If there are certain people who seem to always make you feel less-than (like seeing pics of your ex-boyfriend's new girlfriend), unfollow immediately. Out of sight, out of mind.

Glow Girl Affirmation:
I only compare myself to myself.

3

Baby Fat

"When the pain of NOT embracing and honoring our bodies is greater than embracing our magnificent bodies as vehicles of our souls, that's when we change—not a second before."

—Emme

ALWAYS WONDERED WHAT the cut-off age is for your baby, when you can't say your pregnancy-related muffin top is just "baby fat."

Why did I feel so compelled to justify my new-found jolliness? What did it matter? I had a living miracle that I created in my body. My vessel that craved buckets of egg salad and milkshakes. I mean, I was eating for two. And after all, I was going to be bringing another human into this world. This is an incredible feat. I *deserve* whatever I want! And that's exactly what I did. I think my husband was boiling a dozen eggs every morning before leaving for work so that I would have enough egg salad to last me through the day…or at least till noon! I was obsessed.

My indulgence kind of backfired. And front-fired (is it possible to side-fire?). I gained sixty pounds, front and back, and let's be real—all over. I was somehow under the impression that once I gave birth that the extra fifty pounds would come out with the baby. Yeah…that didn't happen. Actually, just the opposite. Somehow even sans the baby, I managed to gain more weight.

Now what? What was this? Baby fat. The baby fat that never went away.

I remember one day being out with my dad and son when he was around ten years old and we were sitting at a table eating ice cream cones (no, they were not egg-salad flavor— *gross!*) and I got into a conversation about my weight with my dad and shared my frustration. I told him that even if I work out and eat less, it just never seemed to go away. He seemed confused too and said that he noticed I barely ate anything. I said, "I know it's so *frustrating*," with an aggravated tone and I suddenly felt a tap on my arm from my son. I turned towards him and he had a sad look on his face. I thought something happened to his ice cream cone, but instead he said, "Do you wish you never had me?" Ugh. So, crushing and heartbreaking. Just stab me in the heart. I didn't even realize he was listening. Of course, I just about burst into tears and immediately looked directly in his eyes and said, "Absolutely not. The day you were born was the happiest day of my life. You are a blessing." And the honest truth is I would trade *all* the pounds in the world to have him. Thankfully, a huge ice cream covered smile emerged and I breathed a sigh of relief and squeezed him tight.

This was a huge eye-opener for me. Did I gain this weight with my pregnancy? Yes. Would I do it all over again? In a heartbeat! The most important thing was that I was blessed with my brilliant, smart, funny, compassionate son who stole my heart and changed my life. Beyond that, does it really matter? That's when I began to get comfortable in my own skin. My body created this wonderful little human and I could look at my body now and embrace my muffin top, my C-section scar, and the extra pounds that weren't there before. I felt proud!

But I'm going to be completely honest with you. This is still a work in progress for me as I'm writing this, but I do know now that it takes a healthier mindset and the desire to want to change. Not a quick fix. Trust me, I struggled with this for years. Trying to find the quick fix to make my "baby fat" disappear? Mistake.

How many of you have tried those fad diets, like "eat the most terrible tasting cabbage soup for ten days," or "drink the juice of one hundred grapefruits?" Like you're up late at night after eating a half of pint of Ben & Jerry's Chunky Monkey ice cream (ahem…the whole pint) and suddenly an infomercial pops on the TV and you swear they're talking to *you*. They say, *you* can look like this and we have the quick fix solution for you! You want to dial in right away and get the added low-calorie cookbook for free if you order within the next twenty minutes. Did you dial-in? Did they work?

The key to feeling good is to forget the fad diets and strive to live a healthy lifestyle. And it can't be negative or a deprivation. It must be positive and a mission of self-care, both mind and body.

Now that my son is nineteen, do I still carry some of that "baby fat" nineteen years later? You bet! But I also accept who I am and set goals now to be more fit. I've struggled with feeling comfortable in my own skin, but there are ways of handling it so you don't end up in a downward spiral of negativity and shame.

Imagine if we obsessed about the things we love about ourselves.

There isn't anything more confident and sexier than a woman who is comfortable in her own skin. Big skin, small skin, light skin, dark skin (it almost sounds like a Dr. Seuss book). You get where I'm going with this. It's all beautiful and the confidence is what makes us shine. It's not about how we look; it's about how we *feel*. Our skin doesn't define who we are, our inside does. And seriously, think about it, if we were *all* skinny how interesting would that be?

Perfection is overrated. There is always something to strive for, but it doesn't need to be perfection. No one is perfect, sister. Stop putting unnecessary pressure on yourself. And getting strong doesn't just start with working out, it's about working *in* too. In your head.

I learned that working from the inside out is key. A healthy outside starts from the inside. When feelings have not been addressed, they start to "pile" on.

There are many excuses we give ourselves for not making our health a priority. Like "I don't have time" or "it's too expensive" or "I'm too tired." But have you ever said to yourself that you are not working out or eating healthy because you're...scared?

Change is scary, even when we know it's good for us.

You might wonder, "what would life be like if I were skinnier?"

If you're feeling uncertain or nervous about taking that first step, know that you're not alone. You need to uncover what is "weighing" you down and I guarantee you'll discover things within yourself that could change your entire life.

One of the challenges that I faced in creating my new healthy lifestyle was completely unexpected. I strongly desired to be in better shape and eat as healthy as possible. I felt I was in the right mindset, so I forged forward. Little did I know, the challenge that showed up wasn't relating to me *maintaining* this new lifestyle. As soon as I saw progress being made, I became excited imagining my new "self" and how great I would feel physically. But what I didn't expect was every time I had a positive thought about my progress, right after the feeling of excitement, I started to feel intense anxiety. Anxiety isn't something that I deal with on a regular basis so when it happens, I know it's coming from somewhere so deep I didn't even know it was there. Through some intense self-discovery, I had the realization that I had been subconsciously holding on to my baby fat (inside) even though I kept saying I wanted to be fit and feel better (outside). I was working from the outside in, rather than working from the inside out.

I was wearing an armor to protect myself. This "armor" creates a protective barrier between you and people in the world who can make you feel vulnerable. As I'm writing this now, I am on my healthy lifestyle journey and slowly my pieces of armor have been falling off. It's a feeling of true vulnerability. It's still a little scary to imagine how I might feel once all the pieces are gone, but I'm focusing on my progress and not worrying about the unknown.

Through my journey, what really helped was writing a love letter saying goodbye to my "armor." I know this might sound a little cray-cray, but it works. If there is something you've been holding onto but know you are ready to release it, write it a letter to say farewell.

Dear Armor (aka Baby Fat),

Thank you for protecting me. You have been there by my side through all my struggles. You've insulated me and you've comforted me. I'm so grateful for your support and shelter, but I feel strong now. It's become tiring carrying you around. You're cumbersome and while I know you're guarding me from any possible hurt, you are weighing me down. And I know as you go piece by piece, a little more light will shine. And when you are gone, I will be ready to fly.

Don't let the idea of change scare you as much as the prospect of remaining unhappy.

We cannot change our past or our genes but what we can do is understand it and give ourselves compassion. And once we take away our own shame, the expectations and stereotypes we have been bombarded with diminishes and we can begin to let go of all the internal beliefs we told ourselves over the years and release any protective barriers we may be carrying.

Wouldn't this feel liberating and wonderful?

I've learned that while we need to be proud of who we are, it's also important to feel healthy. They are two different things. Do I want to be fit and in shape now because that's the way I think women should look? Absolutely not.

I love to dance so instead of trying to follow a work-out routine (that I ultimately can never seem to follow), I just put on my favorite music and dance for thirty minutes. And I dance like no one is watching! Doing something you love makes all the difference. Like I said, it's all in the mindset. I don't care about weighing myself, but I do care how I feel, and I strive to be healthy. If I feel energetic and spunky with lots of energy, that means more to me than any number on a scale.

When you start taking care of yourself, you start feeling better and doing better.

Now I do things that are fun, make me happy, and embrace my "baby fat." It's like a big tattoo that proudly says, "Mom!"

I was one of those women who knew I wanted to have a baby. I got married shortly after I turned thirty, so I wanted to start trying right away. Within months, we found out we were pregnant. I still remember that feeling once we found out that a human life was growing inside me. It gave me this huge sense of responsibility that I never felt before. It was like nothing I had ever experienced. I thought, *I'm responsible right now for this baby growing inside me and I have to make every decision wisely.* We let friends and family know and since I'm the only child my parents were elated to hear they were going to have a grandchild.

Then one day I began to bleed. With my heart pounding out of my chest I went to see my doctor to find out I miscarried. WTF? *How could this be?* I thought. I was completely devastated—lifeless. I laid in bed for days and days and was in the most unreal depression. I didn't even know what was going on.

Why did we buy a crib that I had to walk by every time I managed to get myself up out of bed to get a glass of water?

Why did I have Baby Gap clothes folded neatly on my dresser? Why was everyone calling me when I didn't want to talk? What did I do wrong?

I didn't know anything about miscarriages and how common they were, especially in first pregnancies. I felt so alone and damaged. I seriously didn't know how I could go on. I think about women who struggle with infertility as my mind automatically went down that path after I miscarried and it's heartbreaking.

I finally got the strength to move on one small step at a time. I wrote a farewell love letter to my "baby". Learning more about miscarriages and connecting with other moms who had gone through similar experiences and still had multiple children gave me hope. Connecting and sharing. Supporting and bonding. Eventually my "why me" turned into "why *not* me?" I told you that this saying is one of my faves!

Shortly after, I became pregnant again and I was blessed with my son. The process of becoming a mom for me, while challenging at first, ultimately led to a stronger sense of self. Being a mom forced me to confront many issues and obstacles and be strong for him, which has also meant finding ways to be strong for myself.

We need to love ourselves and embrace our physical uniqueness (aka flaws). Are you wondering, *Love myself? What? I don't even like myself most days!* I hear you girl! I'm right there with you and struggle with this too.

Accept imperfection. Embrace it. The most beautiful, confident women are those who own their unique look and refuse to apologize. Being comfortable in your own skin is about knowing who you are and being okay with it. A true sense of self and acceptance of who you are and knowing you are perfectly imperfect is the most freeing feeling in the world.

Do you remember when you were little and hated something physical about yourself, like your hair or your height? Like me,

I hated my fire engine red hair and freckles. But as I got older, I realized this is what makes me, me. This is my uniqueness and I should be proud of it. Embrace those so-called flaws that make you who you are with grace. Everyone has something they don't like about themselves, but that "flaw" is often what makes you interesting, unique, and beautiful.

I can't tell you how many times since I gained my "baby fat" that I've said things like, "I'm so fat," "I hope they don't take my picture," "If I was only skinnier…" What happens when we say things like this to ourselves? We drown in negative body image. And it can be anything that triggers this. Walking by a mirror or pants that just came out of the dyer (sisters, I know many of you can relate to this!). Think of all the time we spend doing this to ourselves when we could be giving ourselves loving, positive affirmations.

Accept your body in this moment. Feeling comfortable in our own skin has its rewards. Imagine how different your life can be in this very moment if you stop trying to berate, change, or control your body and instead allow yourself to accept your body for what it is. You won't let any sideways glances or comments affect you. You will be objective and not take things personal. What a freeing feeling! If you love yourself inside *and* outside, you will open the door to many wonderful experiences you might have otherwise missed.

When we accept, we let go of the struggle. We let go of perfection. When the ideal is being "perfect," it creates a barrage of self-doubt, anxiousness, and low self-esteem—everything that keeps us from living life with confidence, courage, and fierceness. It's not about trying to be perfect. It is about accepting the fact that you aren't perfect, and neither is anyone else.

Get rid of the belief that the only way to look is like a model. We are *all* models. All beautiful, lovely, unique shaped models. We need to get rid of all the self-defeating thoughts so we can rise up to be the beautiful person God made. If we don't, we are doing ourselves an injustice.

I love this quote from Jenna Blush Hager: "Who I am is more important than how I look. If I radiate love, kindness, and empathy, I can bring some light into this dark world—and isn't that better than being a size zero?"

It's been a journey for me and I'm so grateful that I learned to build confidence inside and eventually outside. When I think back to all the mean, hurtful things I said to myself it breaks my heart. Why would I allow this? Why did I feel this was the only option? Year after year saying negative things to myself and feeling less than. Making the decision to love myself has changed my life.

I am consciously making healthier decisions and doing something active every day. I created a healthy way of living because I matter. Because I love myself enough to care. And this all started with accepting myself for who I am along with all my "flaws" and releasing my armor. My mindset has shifted. This isn't about dieting to look a certain way. This isn't about depriving myself to be skinny. This isn't about dreading to exercise. This is a whole new way of thinking and being. I'm so excited about my new lifestyle. If you stop body shaming and create a new mindset, things will change for you too.

I am a huge believer of positive affirmations. I tell myself every day, *I enjoy feeling fit.* This motivates me to do something active and inspires me to continue to maintain my healthy lifestyle. Imagine if I said something like, *I look like a fat cow* (yes, I've gone there!), *I guess I better work out.* Does that sound very motivating? No, it sounds like I should hide in bed with a box of Double Stuf Oreos. It's all about being in a positive mindset.

Do I eat kale chips and granola every day? No, I eat what I want keeping in mind that I want to be healthy. I drink a ton of water (which is so important) and eat lots of fruits and veggies, but I also eat pasta, bread, and chocolate because I love them. I mean, come on, who can possibly live without chocolate? It's all in moderation and not about deprivation.

I used to make homemade ice cream with my dad when I was little and it's my all-time favorite. It's not only nostalgic, but it tastes so delicious (damn you, ice cream!). Could I eat it every day? Absolutely. But I know that's not going to fit in with my healthy lifestyle. Do I still eat it occasionally? Sure do! But that's okay. I make the decisions and I know what works best for me and deprivation is *not* part of my lifestyle. If it's a friend's birthday and we are all having ice cream and cake, I'm in. It's time to celebrate! At the same time, I also have the mindset now when I look at a yummy brownie ice cream sundae, I can either choose to eat it or I can choose to be healthy. Hmm... when I put it like that, *I choose* the latter. I do quite a bit of self-talk, which is not unusual for me!

Don't deprive yourself of certain things, because then you will become fixated on them. Have what you want in moderation and get active doing something you love.

When I work out (dance), I pump myself up ahead of time, reminding myself how great I'm going to feel afterwards. I love music and it's a huge motivator for me. I created a playlist with all my favorite uplifting and empowering songs. Once I hit "play," there's seriously no turning back. Now instead of dreading it, I look forward to it; I welcome it.

These are all things I choose for myself now. Because I love me. Even with all the "flaws."

Learn to embrace things about your body in a different light. With grace. I hated being in a bathing suit because of my legs. They don't have any shape to them. I even had a nickname for them—TT's. That works with Thunder Thighs or Tree Trunks; pick your poison. Every time I looked at them, I'd say, "I hate my legs." *Now* I've learned to appreciate them because they may not be shapely or perfect, but they are perfectly imperfect. They are strong and they've carried me through many challenges in life, they've happily danced, they've picked me up when I've fallen and I'm grateful for them. I've made it to where I am today because of these legs.

Love all of you. Like Ashley Graham says, "Rolls, curves, cellulite—all of it. I love every part of me. I believe that beauty is beyond size."

I'm curvy and I *own* that now. My body is one big beautiful roadmap of all my struggles and accomplishments, and it tells a story. And as I get stronger and fitter in my mind and body, I stand taller with more confidence. I feel better about myself and appreciate all that my body has achieved. I'm grateful that even though I didn't love my body, it still loved me back.

You need to get rid of the idea that you can never be thin enough, attractive enough, or whatever negative thoughts you are telling yourself.

I love this: The beautiful light behind her smile makes her eyes *glow* with a love for life I've never experienced before. What true beauty is.

You are beautiful as you are. Your curves, words, thoughts, strengths, flaws. You are magic, so own your glow! Let go of the struggle. Stop the negative body shaming, be gentle and kind to yourself, and accept your body in all of its glory! Every scar, wrinkle, birthmark, piece of cellulite, beauty mark, and freckle is a beautiful tapestry interwoven over time to tell a powerful, magical, and miraculous story of how you survived and thrived…and glowed in the face of it all.

A few of my favorite tips to reclaim yourself...

1. When you start to hear those negative thoughts about how you look, stop the self-hate and go to self-love. Remember these are your thoughts, not fact. It's up to you to act. Instead of focusing on how your body looks on the outside, think about all the positive attributes your body has from the inside. What are they? Make a list and be grateful for them. Keep this list handy so you can reflect when needed.

2. When body image or motherhood issues arise, the last thing you probably want to do is be around others. I have found that surrounding myself with positive people in my life helps because it gets me out of my head. Feeling connected with others can squash some of the perfectionism and criticism tied to body dissatisfaction and self-worth.

3. In moments when body image issues come up, I am usually feeling critical in some way about myself. If I dig deep, most of the time I realize it is not about my body. My body is just the go-to negative coping mechanism I utilize in the moment. What I need most when I am feeling and focusing negatively about my body or myself is to treat myself with kindness. Beating myself up will not help me but doing something nice for myself that pertains to self-care will. If you must focus on a body part, do it with compassion and get massage, facial, manicure...or all of the above!

Glow Girl Affirmation:
My imperfections make me unique.

4

Cocktails & Confetti

"The more you praise and celebrate your life, the more there is in life to celebrate."

—*Oprah Winfrey*

W HY COCKTAILS & Confetti? They both make me happy! I love cocktails and I love to entertain, and I believe we should look at every day like a celebration. When we wake up each day, we have an entire day ahead of us to design our day—to create, build our dream, discover, and live our purpose. Isn't that something to celebrate?

Add all the different "ingredients" and mix it up like a cocktail!

Life is a celebration. A celebration of gratitude for simply being alive every day! Imagine that feeling when you see confetti floating down around you. How do you feel? Happy, playful, joyous? Where does all the fear we hold go at that moment; all the self-doubt and those negative thoughts that are always looming over us? My purpose is to help show that we can all live like that every day!

When I was living my life constantly comparing my life to others, how was I truly living my life? I wasn't. How could I enjoy the life I was living when I was looking at other people living their lives? Wishing I had something like them. I think about the moments I must have missed. At one point I decided

I couldn't watch other people's lives while my own passed me by.

This life happens once and it's going fast like a runaway train. In the blink of an eye, ten years go by and we have no idea where it went. Now is the moment we have. We have no idea what tomorrow holds. So, jump on the party train!

Experiences have happened in my life that reminded me that life is short, so live now and live out loud. Once I started putting myself out there and focusing on my special talents, the more I wanted to share my life with other people. The mind shift went from isolating myself because I didn't want to see what great lives other people had, to wanting to share my life.

My love for entertaining came from one spur of the moment Cinco de Mayo party. I still remember calling a friend years ago and asking her opinion on what she thought about me hosting a party for a few of our neighborhood friends. Cinco de Mayo = excuse to drink margaritas! She thought it was an awesome idea and the Annual Cinco De Mayo party was born that next weekend. It has continued annually for over twelve years now. It started with a few neighbors and now it's up to over sixty people!

The feeling of celebrating life with all my friends was something I knew needed to be a bigger part of my life moving forward. This was the start of me being more open and sharing my love for entertaining and my home with others. We all looked forward to it every year and my house became known as the "Cinco De Mayo Party House." I loved to create different margaritas but had trouble finding interesting mixers. That's when I decided to make my own. I created watermelon margaritas, mango margaritas, and blackberry margaritas all made with fresh ingredients. They were a hit! Everyone loved them and would continually tell me how great they were throughout the night. Maybe a little too great. That's what I'm usually told the next day!

I believe this was the start of my beverage career. It's so interesting to see how each of our passions come to light. If you've been working on trying to discover your passion but feel stuck, stop trying. When we stop trying to force it, somehow it surfaces on its own. We need to be ready to see it and embrace it. It might be right in front of you and you don't know it.

I know when I'm passionate about something because it's when it doesn't feel like work. Once it starts feeling like work, it's time to explore a new passion—which is perfectly fine. Moving from one passion to another doesn't mean you failed. One passion could lead you to another which is what I discovered. There's not one single chapter.

I would always say, "I'm getting there," somehow to make myself feel better that I'm making progress. But where exactly was I going? What was my final destination? It's not about the destination and I know that now. I worked so hard to grow my beverage brand and I thought if we can just get the brand in stores nationally then we would be successful. Would that then be my final destination? No, because here I am on this new path now. Life is a journey and we need to celebrate each step of the way not just at the end when we think we "made it."

Everyone has a different meaning of success. We see people with big homes, fancy clothes, luxury-vehicles, and most people think, *now* they've made it. But have they? What's their story? Are they happy?

While it seems we all strive to gain material things, many of us are searching for authentic experiences. Something that goes beyond the material world. It may be a deep connection, finding your purpose, or something spiritual. And at the core of all of these experiences, there's one common thread. It's about attaining some kind of a "feeling" we are striving for.

A celebration is exactly about that. It evokes a feeling within us that we all crave in our lives. It's when we can find something we are grateful for or passionate about and share it with others.

What makes you want to celebrate?

Happiness derived from material things quickly fades over time. When we buy something it immediately makes us happy, right? But then what happens over time? It's exciting at first, but then it seems to fade into the background of our lives. It becomes just a blur. With experiences, they become part of who we are, part of our identity, which brings us greater satisfaction and ultimately happiness.

We are the sum total of our experiences and the people we surround ourselves with.

I did an exercise a few months ago. I started writing down things that made me happy. I loved it so much that I continue to add to it and often. I carry this around with me in a little notebook (you can use your phone to keep notes too).

Here's an excerpt from my "Happiness Journal":

The sound of rain outside my window
My morning smoothie
Fresh cut grass
Birds chirping at the start of spring
Conversations with my son
The angels in my life
London
A crackling fire
Meeting someone new
An elderly couple holding hands
Driving with my moonroof open
The sound of waves crashing
Meeting Earth, Wind & Fire
Inspiring someone
My Spotify song lists
Hugs

I encourage you to give this a try. What is your happiness? Big or small.

For me, I started to *notice* things more and became more aware of little things that might have otherwise passed me by. It caused me to value and appreciate what I currently have as opposed to the things I seem to continually strive for. It made me stop thinking that I can't appreciate the now until I reach my goals. It changed my mindset to live in the moment and appreciate my journey.

Are some of the things on my list "celebration" worthy? Maybe not to have a party or a ceremony, but certainly meaningful enough to "celebrate" every second of it.

So, let's take one thing from my list. Meeting Earth, Wind & Fire. All my friends know that EWF is my all-time favorite band. Seriously (I know, I'm dating myself here). But who can't smile when you hear their song, September? That's some get up and dance music! I hear it now in my head and I'm smiling… *come on!* Anywho, so, I have EWF albums (yes, I said albums). All of them. I have an EWF t-shirt and ticket stubs to the live concerts. I even have an original signed photo I bought at their concert in New York City.

I love my EWF memorabilia, but would all these things combined top seeing them perform? No. I would trade it all in to see them in person. Why? The experience. The experience of hearing them play, dancing in the aisle, singing all the words, clapping and cheering, meeting other super fans, and feeling the happiness that exudes all around me while I'm there. Living in the moment and taking it all in.

The last EWF concert I went to a couple of years ago for my birthday, I decided to be bold. It's about the experience, right? I made the decision to rush down to the front of the stage. I wasn't sure what was going to happen, but I somehow knew it would be worth the risk. I thought *I'm old-ish now,* what would security do to me? I made it down past security and my friends followed behind me. We did it! We made it to the stage. They were larger than life and I was loving it. There I was singing my head off when one of the guitarists looked over at me. *Wait, was he looking right at me?* Yes, he was and then...wait for it...he smiled! He smiled at me! Seriously! And then just when I thought it couldn't get any better, a guy with an EWF jacket came up to us and handed us three backstage passes to meet the band. *What? I must be dreaming*, I thought. I cried tears of joy. This was a dream come true and there is not a material thing that could replace that night. That night will always be a part of me.

Celebration transforms something ordinary into something special.

Experiences open us up to a new world. Things we might not see or feel otherwise. Things that help shape and inspire us. Perhaps even change your life or bless us with a beautiful memory that we never could even imagine (more on that in another chapter, but no skipping ahead!).

It was always my dream to go to Europe and about five years ago I finally visited London. The experience was magical. I was seeing things in person that I had only seen in movies. The London Eye, Big Ben, corner English Pubs. I was so grateful to have had the opportunity to go and I will forever celebrate my time in London.

These might be external things, but the gratefulness (and the happiness that results) comes from within. So, take time to notice and appreciate everything around us, and everyone we see and interact with.

Take a moment and look closely at things around you. What do you see that makes you happy? Something in nature, a book, a cup of coffee, a comfortable chair, a fluffy blanket?

These are all things to celebrate.

While we think that having a party is the only way to celebrate, there are many other ways. A celebration is taking time to pause and appreciate any moment or event in your life. This is your time to celebrate the moments or events that make you happy, your accomplishments, to celebrate *you*. It's a time to be grateful for where you've been, where you are, and where you're going. Your journey.

A celebration can be sharing a joyful experience with loved ones or simple pleasures.

Don't *wait* for the right "occasion" to celebrate and enjoy life. You choose the moments, events, and experiences. You will begin to notice the shift into your perception towards life.

The day my son was born was by far the most magical moment to celebrate! He truly was a miracle after twelve hours of labor and C-section. I was so blessed that he came into my life healthy and he instantly stole my heart. Quite a lot has happened over the past nineteen years since he entered my life. With my marriage, my business, personal development, the ups and downs of everyday life, but the one constant throughout all of this has been my amazing, smart, funny son.

He is my favorite person and over the past few years, as he was entering the "teens," I was nervous that this incredible bond that we had might change. Of course, the relationship changed as he changed, but the bond has remained constant. I am truly grateful.

About a little over a year ago I asked him if he wanted to go out for lunch on a Saturday. I remember that day vividly and how great I felt when we got home. That we had uninterrupted time together, no housework, no bills, no emails, no dog, no distractions. I saw how valuable that was and I spontaneously asked him, "Hey, how about we make this a thing? How about we do this every weekend when I'm not traveling?" It was kind of scary putting myself out there in the "teen world" asking my seventeen-year-old son to spend time with his mom, but to my pleasant surprise he quickly answered, "Sure."

This was one of the best decisions that I've made because it has allowed us to spend hours and hours of uninterrupted time over this past year and as each month passes, I think to myself maybe this will wear off and he'll get bored with the whole idea. But I realized that he looks forward to this time together as much as I do, and it fills my heart.

Everyone is so busy in this world right now with all that's going on, crazy work hours, kids, emails, social media, and just everyday life hitting us at every angle. So today—take time to talk. Take the time, uninterrupted with someone special in your life. Even if it's once a month, it's priceless and unlike material things, you will always have those memories.

These are moments to celebrate.

My life wasn't exactly heading in the direction I expected, but that doesn't mean there still aren't moments to celebrate. Every setback is an opportunity to test your self-reliance. That's why you have to celebrate adversity. Without it, you will never rise to your greatness.

Choose to become joyful. Each moment is precious and fragile. Expected or unexpected. We are so fortunate to have these moments when so many others are denied moments.

One of my favorite quotes from Mandy Hale: "True happiness is letting go of what we think our life is supposed to look like and celebrating it for everything that it is."

When we celebrate even the tiniest moments of life, we bring awareness and focus on these wonderful feelings and attract even more special moments into our lives. Celebrating our wins, big or small, allows us to acknowledge our accomplishments and propels us to keep going. Who wouldn't want more celebrations? (I'm raising my hand right now!)

And don't diminish your wins either. Then how will you get to celebrate if you say, *it wasn't that big of a deal—it sounds like I'm bragging.* When we diminish or fear what other people will say, then we are not living out our purpose. Be proud. Share your zest for life!

While I'm now someone who doesn't need an excuse to have a good time, I realize that celebration is largely lacking in our everyday lives. Think about how you want to celebrate. Champagne, a trip, a dinner at your favorite restaurant, snuggle on the couch with your kids? Or maybe play your jam with the volume high and have a personal dance party? (Yep, I've done that.)

So, stay open, keep experimenting, keep making progress, and celebrate everything along the way. Hell, I decided to celebrate after every chapter I completed writing this book!

Parties were usually a big deal for me growing up. That was my mom's department. She always managed to create special birthday parties for me that had a creative twist—whether it was Cookie Monster cake with blue dyed coconut for "fur," or a magical treasure hunt party with maps to guide us on a quest through the woods to find a treasure chest loaded with goodies, to my teen Shawn Cassidy themed party. They were all special. The sensation of feeling special, feeling love, friendship, and joy all made the celebration memorable. I, in turn, did the same for my son's birthdays.

As an adult, I loved the sense of community I felt when I hosted a party. Connecting and celebrating were my passions that found me at my party. I was passionate about people! I found it strange that my passion was people when I've always been shy. Sometimes you can't force it—let it come to you. You never know where "it" might be coming from. You could have the realization from one experience or event.

I love this: life is kind of like a party. You invite a lot of people, some leave early, some stay all night, some laugh with you, some laugh at you, and some show up really late. But in the end, after the fun, there are a few who stay to help clean up the mess. And most of the time they aren't even the ones who made the mess. These people are your true friends in life. They are the only ones who matter.

Only party with people who celebrate life.

Celebrate the people that have come into your life to help you weave the tapestry of your unique and beautiful story. Each successful step of the way; celebrate with them. We are working so hard to get to where we want to go, we don't stop to smell the roses on the way. Enjoy the journey.

Life turns into a celebration when you begin to enjoy every moment of it. I began to love life and it loved me back. You don't need anybody else except yourself to turn your life into a celebration. Soon you will notice that the world responds to your celebration and will become a part of it. Say "yes" to life and live it fully.

I love this quote from Rajneesh, with my special twist: "Life should be a continual celebration, a festival of lights the whole year round. Only then can you *glow* up, can you blossom."

There's always a reason to celebrate. Find it. Share it. Toss some confetti in the air and start living life like every day is a celebration!

A few of my favorite tips to help you celebrate life (and a bonus cocktail recipe—woot woot!)...

1. Take a break from technology at least once a day for five minutes. Think about your wins, big or small. Like you landed a big account or got them through the morning successfully getting your kids off to school. There must be at least one thing, right? Then look any miracles you see around you. Like an uplifting story you heard or the sun glistening on the fall leaves. Now how can we not want to celebrate every day?

2. Find one moment of magic in every day. This moment can be simple or profound. Like taking that first bite of a cheesy pizza and how the cheese stretches from the slice to your mouth, or the way the sunlight glistens on

fresh falling snow, or a friend calling you just when you needed it. Once you see or feel it, take a snapshot of that moment in your mind. These precious moments are stored away for you to access at any time.

3. Create a celebration! Make one of my specialty cocktails or a mocktail and make a toast with a friend or friends who have been by your side and celebrate your friendship and life! Dance (you can see by now this is my thing!) and sing as you create this moment worthy of celebration. AND as a special bonus I'm sharing one of my favorite recipes with you; so, cheers!

COCKTAIL RECIPE:
Glow Girl Gimlet

(For a mocktail just exclude the Gin or Vodka)

This cucumber cocktail is so refreshing and delicious! One sip, and you'll be glowing!

Ingredients - per cocktail

- ☐ 2 slices of peeled cucumber, quartered
- ☐ 5-8 mint leaves
- ☐ 1 ½ teaspoons light agave nectar or simple syrup
- ☐ 1/2 lime, juiced
- ☐ 1 ½ ounces Gin (or Vodka)

INSTRUCTIONS :

1. In a cocktail shaker muddle the cucumber, mint, and agave nectar until the cucumber is tender.

2. Fill the shaker with ice, then pour in the lime juice and gin. Put the lid on your shaker and shake until the cocktail is thoroughly chilled, about 15 seconds.

3. Strain the mixture into a martini glass. Garnish with a tiny sprig of mint.

Mix it up! Substitute basil for mint, and/or add a little splash of elderflower liqueur, and/or muddle some fresh jalapeño with the cucumber. You could also make this cocktail on the rocks and add a little ginger beer.

P.S. If no one is free to help you celebrate just let me know, I am always ready to party (just ask my friends)!

Glow Girl Affirmation:
I am worth celebrating.

5

Sipping A Dream

"If I have the belief that I can do it, I shall surely acquire the capacity to do it even if I may not have it at the beginning."

— *Gandhi*

THE IDEA OF my beverage brand all started with a passion. A passion for creating, entertaining, and wanting to find *my* passion. As they say, when you are handed lemons make lemonade (or lemon-flavored cocktails in my case)! When I was laid off from a corporate job ten years prior, I went back to the beginning. What was my passion? How had I forgotten? Did I ever actually know what my passion was? It was time for me to go back to the beginning.

I knew I couldn't bear the drudgery of another corporate job. I needed something more creative and I was determined to find it. I just didn't know what I was looking for. So, I knew I loved to create. I loved entertaining and making fresh innovative cocktails…but what could I do with that? Have lots of parties? That could be fun, but there was only so much my liver could take. And the purpose, *my* newfound purpose, was to find something I was passionate about that could make money—not cost money!

I was fortunate to have an incredible group of friends and family. After countless inspiring conversations with my friends,

I knew there had to be something there...something relating to creating, mixing, and entertaining. After doing loads of research, I saw a growing niche; one that I was already creating in my home entertaining with natural and organic cocktails! *Ah ha! That's it! I will be the one who can help people entertain naturally, but with style too! Eco-chic!* I set out to write a book and create a website called ECO-BAR. I designed a logo and built the informational website myself. I wrote my book proposal until the wee hours, sometimes only sleeping between two and three hours a night.

I was on a mission. Without a salary, I only had so long to make something work before I would need to get a job to pay my bills. Yeah...no pressure, right? I completed my 100-page eco-entertaining book proposal and began sending it off to literary agents. In the meantime, I was building up my website. People found it and were intrigued. They didn't realize there were a growing number of organic spirits out on the market. I was educating people and sharing information that benefited them and I loved it. I wanted to do more.

I heard of an upcoming "green" festival in Philly and for a brief moment thought this would be cool to go and show off my ECO-BAR concept. Then the reasonable voice inside my head said, *what are you thinking? You don't even have a business! Do you have a booth, and swag to put in your booth? You don't even have business cards! Don't be foolish!* I thought it was my reasonable voice, but it was that pesky Negative Nancy again.

You know, when we start to think we can do something for a fleeting moment...there it is, making us doubt ourselves, essentially creating fear. Fear holds us back and if you can acknowledge that and break through even temporarily, it can help you take that next little step and that's exactly what I did. My acronym for fear is: Face. Everything. And. Rise.

The day before the festival, I was considering going to the shore because it was going to be a beautiful weekend. As I was thinking about how going to the beach wasn't going to help propel me, I had this overwhelming feeling that I needed to go to the festival. The doubt escaped me for the moment, and I was excited for what seemed like an incredible opportunity. I called and negotiated a booth space (there was ONE left) and it was 5 p.m. the night before. I had nothing to go with. I had a website, but how do you show that? When in doubt… go to Target! I (literally) ran through the store trying to find anything that looked, "ECO-BAR." In a mad dash I found two bookcases that could work as a bar, two funky looking bar stools, glasses, napkins, and a bowl that screamed "organic" that I filled with fresh bright orange clementines.

Doing the festival was scary, but I felt like it was what I wanted and where I should have been. We were fortunate to have a great space under a tree and it was a beautiful, sunny fall day. Everyone was drawn to our bar. It was thrilling to see so many people interested in what I was doing, even if they were just hoping to get a cocktail! People asked lots of questions mostly: "when are you going to open an ECO-BAR?" I offered catering services and promoted my website, but in my gut, I knew I was onto something bigger.

After the event, I felt an adrenaline rush of inspiration! It was like nothing I had ever experienced before. So many people wanted to learn about what I was doing… but *I* needed to figure out what exactly that was! I was able to get a few cocktail catering events from that festival and my creations were making people happy. I knew I was moving in the right direction.

During this period, I had the good sense to take one step at a time and not try to map out the entire journey from the beginning. Usually I'm a planner but this process was different. "Don't judge each day by the harvest you reap, but by the seeds you plant;" a quote from Robert Lewis Stevenson had special meaning for me. I was giving myself permission to plant seeds.

The one thing I knew was that I loved talking about how

the cocktails were made and showing people how they could create them. People loved the fresh flavors and unique combinations. After a year of hearing, *wow, you are so talented*, and *how did you come up with these flavors*; I had my lightbulb moment. I could create a bottled beverage! I wasn't sure if it would be with or without alcohol, but it had to be creative, all-natural, organic, lightly sweetened, and nothing artificial. First, I wanted a name and then a "look." I love design, so this was fun for me. I researched thousands of beverage names and bottles online and was drawn to simple names and designs. "Sip" resonated with me. Adding the extra "p" was to add a little flair and I could trademark it.

After researching costs, I knew I had to create a non-alcoholic brand. The costs were less, and I liked the idea of creating a specialty beverage for people who don't drink alcohol yet could be versatile enough to serve as a cocktail mixer.

Voila, the idea of Sipp was born!

Next was to work on the flavors… I liked the idea of adding multiple flavors in one bottle like an instant cocktail. The idea came to me at an event where I was making Blackberry Mojitos. Everyone wanted to make one at home but when I started to explain how, I couldn't get past "muddle three blackberries," let alone the four other ingredients to create it before their eyes would glaze over with a deer in the headlights look. "I need to buy ALL those ingredients just to make one cocktail?" was the usual response. That was it! My beverage needed to be more than all-natural; it had to be a combination of flavors to make it easy for people and more cost effective. My first flavor idea was blackberry, mint, and lime called Mojo Berry based on the cocktail, mojito. I worked on many more flavor combinations and loved every minute of it.

This is going to be great, I thought. *I will create a beverage everyone will love, and it will be in stores, hotels, and restaurants. Easy-peasy.* Uh…yeah, not so much.

Once I had my concept, I needed to figure how I could go into production on a shoestring. I found a female beverage consultant online. I thought it would be a breeze working with her because she would want to support another woman going into business. Whomp whomp. I was wrong. When I asked if she could help me for a reduced upfront fee, she gave me an emphatic *NO!* Scrooge McHigh-Heels had apparently done this work too many times in the past and seen lots of failures. She then proceeded to warn me that if I didn't have at least a million dollars I might as well forget it and making sure to highlight that 85% of all beverage business fail! She ended with "go to a few beverage conferences. Good luck." Click. Dial tone.

So much for, "female business owners unite." *I should probably listen to her*, I thought. *She is the expert after all.*

I went to bed that night feeling defeated. The next morning was a pivotal point in my journey. I had to believe in *myself.* Even despite what an "expert said," why couldn't I be in the 15% of beverage businesses that succeed? Why did I assume I would fall into the 85%? Then, I got angry! How dare she insinuate I was going to fail. I WILL prove her wrong.

The gift I got from Scrooge McHigh-Heels? I used her doubt in me as fuel to work harder. One naysayer was not going to throw me off track. And my deep burning passion would help me keep the blinders on. Who knows why she was being super negative toward me and maybe she wished she thought of my idea first?

I continued to work on my flavors and reached out to beverage experts I found on the Internet. I was fortunate to find many helpful people along the way who shared information and advice just because they believed in the brand and *me!* Everyone told me I needed a co-packer to bottle my beverage.

What on earth is a co-packer? Hooray for the Internet which has answers to just about anything! We live in an age where lack of knowledge isn't a huge barrier to following your passion. Just "Google" it (LinkedIn and YouTube are pretty handy, too)! Mentorship from complete strangers was another benefit of the internet. There are people who exist in this world who will share information and do good just for the sake of doing good.

Back to the story. I found a co-packer in Pennsylvania and learned that they bottle beverages for many brands. I reached out to them to see about bottling my beverage with my three recipes. They told me I would need to run one thousand cases per flavor, which would cost thousands of dollars. Then, when I explained my little kitchen recipes, I think I heard her stifle a laugh. Apparently, I needed to bring my recipe to a flavor house. *WTF is that? Agh! Back to the internet!* A flavor house is where you bring your recipe to flavor chemists who can translate your kitchen recipe into a large production formula at the low-low price of...$25,000-$30,000 per flavor.

Sadly, I thought that this was the end of Sipp. I didn't have that kind of money. With the loss of my income, we were barely getting by.

I went to bed that night thinking this was too hard, and I would be part of the 85%. I didn't know what I was doing, this would never work, and I didn't have the money to fund it.

And then...I woke up and hit the reset button. I decided to spend one week (the time I had until I would need to start looking for a job) and call every organic flavor house I could find to see if they would be willing to work with me on the payment. I spent countless hours researching companies and contacts.

By the third day, I got in touch with a business development manager of a large flavor house. Somehow, I found his cell phone number on the Internet. I actually reached him and was reticent to pitch my idea, but he was willing to listen. He seemed intrigued and mentioned there was a big natural products expo in California the following week and his company was going to be exhibiting there. If I could get out there and tell my story and share my beverage concept, there could be a chance they would create my flavors at no cost if they believed in it.

California? Next week? Scary. Flight cost, hotel, transportation…how would I actually pull this off? And what if after all that it turns out to be a, "Thanks but no thanks. Best of luck"?

Why is it that we can see the negative so quickly?

I took the first step of at least considering it. How would I ever know if this were possible if I didn't go? I would always wonder—what if? I couldn't live with that. Many of life's failures are people who did not realize how close they were to success when they gave up. I pushed myself to go. It was one of the hardest decisions I had to make. I had to believe in myself again. Once the flight was booked, I continued to second-guess myself, but at that point, I was committed to go! And I summoned every positive affirmation I could think of along the way.

I remember I wanted my husband to go with me so badly because I didn't think I could do this alone. But we could only afford for me to go. When in Los Angeles, I got on the shuttle to bring me to the hotel and it was filled with families. I then realized the convention center I was going to was next to Disneyland. All I could think about on the shuttle was that I wished I was with my family and how much I missed my son. Tears started streaming down my face. This all was way outside my comfort zone.

Once I got to my hotel room I began sobbing again. I called my husband hoping it would calm me down, but it didn't. I needed to pull myself together and get over to the tradeshow and show them my fabulous idea. Then my mind went to what a crazy idea this was. Who does something like this?

Before I left for California, I made some mock bottles with handmade labels and filled them with my three flavors concepts. I then photographed them and designed a postcard with the photo and flavor descriptions. Finally, I created a website and listed it on the postcard: haveasipp.com.

At the convention center while trying to find the flavor house booth, I saw hundreds of beverage companies. How could I make this happen with all this competition? How would my beverage stand out among all the others? I had to shut out the internal and external noise, put my big girl panties on, as they say, and go pitch to this company. Once I got to the booth, everyone I needed to meet was there. We sat at a large table and I was on...and on and on and on!

I began my pitch and talked about how I started, my inspiration, flavor ideas, brand direction, and maybe something about my only flaw was that I cared too much. I dunno; it was a whirlwind. Finally, a voice interrupted Hurricane Beth and said, "Um, we get it and we think it's a great idea. You had us about twenty minutes ago! Most importantly, we believe in YOU. What flavor do you want us to start with?"

I almost fell out of my chair. This was really going to happen! I tried to act calm and cool and be professional by thanking them for the opportunity. They told me that I reminded them of the founder of Honest Tea, who they worked with in the beginning also—a huge compliment.

Once we were done meeting, I walked slowly down the aisle and once I reached the end, I sprinted out to call my husband. "I did it," I yelled before he could even say "hello." It was a massive accomplishment. After all my negative talk before I got there, this showed me I need to have more confidence in myself and see what other people see in me.

People believing in me along my journey gave me strength. The seeds of faith that were given to me by others eventually grew within me.

If I let my self-doubt stop me—and trust me I almost did—my beverage idea would still be just that: an idea. Self-doubt can rear its ugly head every time we venture outside our comfort zone. When we are striving to do something great. Self-doubt never disappears.

I battle with it even today. But the more you put yourself out there, the less it shows up and you get better at overcoming it. Remember, your doubts are only thoughts—not reality and not your future.

One of my favorite quotes is attributed to Honoré de Balzac: "When you doubt your power, you give power to your doubt."

I was so grateful to have this well-respected flavor team behind me and they believed in me enough that they weren't even charging me. That gave me the fuel I needed to persevere because not many people get that kind of opportunity.

My next step was to decide on the first Sipp flavor and to find a bottling plant to make it. Then figure out how to afford to run one thousand cases. This would take thousands of dollars that I didn't have. I knew this would take some creativity. My husband and I decided to talk to his parents about my idea. I created a business plan to present to them and they liked it. More importantly, they believed in *me* and they became Sipp's first investor! I will be forever grateful for them, because without their support I would have never had the opportunity to see my idea come to fruition.

Their investment enabled me to have enough money to go into production with one flavor and attend a tradeshow. I created a budget to ensure we were spending the investment in the best, most cost-effective way.

After lots of deliberation, we finally decided on the ginger, vanilla, and lime flavor. Little did I know this was one of the best decisions I made. I received our first flavor samples and we received three versions to taste against my recipe. We chose the one that was the closest to mine and we officially had our first Sipp flavor.

I worked hard over the next month to plan the production: bottling, caps, labels, UPC codes, ingredients, sweetener, boxes…it was quite the crash course! I signed up for a tradeshow and now we had a deadline. We were all set to run at the bottling plant we chose until they decided at the last minute to raise their minimums to three thousand cases! How could they do this to me? We were only a few weeks away from the tradeshow. This is when I thought it was over. A little strength and perseverance would have to go a long way.

This is one thing I know for sure: You will never accomplish your dreams without a fight. Resistance and obstacles are inevitable, so stay calm and work on a plan. View obstacles as a learning opportunity. Be creative. Sleep on it and look at it with a fresh perspective. Utilize your resources to solve the problem. What connections do you have? Use everything you have at your disposal. Find a space for gratitude when surprises and obstacles come up. Once you overcome them it only makes you stronger. Success is determined at how we view and react to our obstacles.

Have you ever heard of a success story without obstacles? The greater the obstacle, the more glory in overcoming it.

So…I had to find another bottling plant in two days. *I can do this*, I told myself and I did. Now could they work with a small minimum case run and could they fit us in on their schedule before the tradeshow? We were told it was going to be super tight, but they would see what they could do. I needed to order all the ingredients, labels, and caps to keep everything on schedule. Then we got the email. The only date we could finish our order with the bottling plant was the day of the tradeshow setup! How could this happen and more importantly, how could this work all in one day? I thought of all the work I did to get to that point and again I *had* to make it happen.

Then the "what ifs" crept back in playing on a nearly endless loop. But I was determined to make this happen, and I trusted I could come up with a solution.

Having confidence that I could "figure it out" was huge. This helped me get through so many challenging times and to not be as afraid. Trust in yourself. Trust that you can figure it out too. We are women, after all!

While I was working on figuring out production, I realized I had forgotten to create a booth design for the tradeshow. I knew the answer...IKEA! I researched all the pieces at IKEA and drew sketches, priced out everything and after a full day at IKEA—including Swedish meatballs (something just seems wrong about meatballs in a furniture store, but when you are there all day, you have to eat!). I had a real booth.

One of my favorite memories was when I set up my entire booth in my family room and had three of my best friends come over and see it. Their reaction is something I will never forget. Friends can be the biggest support and help propel you forward when you might doubt yourself and I was fortunate to have friends who did just that!

I couldn't wait to show my new brand to the world. It was scary but so exciting. Everything for our production run made one day in advance so we loaded up the U-Haul at $19.99/day van and were on our way. As we were driving over five hours to the bottling plant I remember saying, "Who does this?" I thought I must be insane.

I felt like I was always trying to get "ahead" of fear. I thought if I just kept going it wouldn't have time to catch up to me. I wanted my Sipp brand in the core of my being. I was so motivated and on a mission to learn, grow, evolve, and give back. My passion was driving me fast and fear became smaller and smaller in the review mirror.

We arrived and it was an incredible feeling to look up at that huge old brick building knowing they were going to make *my* beverage that day! When we went in, they had already began batching our ingredients. The flavor was good, just as I had hoped, but it needed to be less sweet. Everyone looked at me and asked what I wanted to do…*like I was an expert*! I had to think quickly because they were on a timeline. They couldn't hold production up for me while I made executive decisions. I decided that we needed to add more ingredients with the exception of the agave so it wouldn't be so sweet.

Did I know it would work? No, but thank God it did, and it was perfect! After we tasted it, it went off to be bottled. It's an indescribable feeling seeing bottles coming down the line that is all your creation. From a little idea to a real product. And it looked good and tasted great. Now I just prayed that everyone else would think so too!

We had hundreds of cases of Sipp Ginger Blossom, a never before seen beverage and we loaded over fifteen cases in our van to try to make it before the end of show set up. The bottles were still hot after being heated up to pasteurize. We made it and set up our booth with the hopes of Sipp being a success.

The next day the show opened…and we were a hit! The people that stopped in our booth and tried Sipp LOVED it. We made some important connections; people who believed in Sipp and me. Many of those people have helped me along the way and I will forever be grateful.

Building my business changed my life. From taking chances, to overcoming so many obstacles, meeting so many brilliant people, creating an outstanding, dedicated, and driven team who became like family to me, to finally believing in myself and my greatness.

The more I grew my business, the more my confidence grew, but Negative Nancy was still there right by my side, waiting for any little failure to pounce on me. Over time, the more supportive people who entered my life, the more she was getting drowned out. And while I was working on switching those negative thoughts to positive, there was nothing more convincing than a new experience to get her to keep quiet.

That's where new beliefs live. And old ones die.

The moment the flavor company chose me. The moment I saw my kitchen-made beverage coming down the production line. The moment I did my first tradeshow. The moment I saw Sipp on the store shelf. The moment I had someone invest in my company. The moment I sold my beverage to Target. The moment I had a team of people. The moment I reached a revenue goal. The moment I won an award for my beverage flavors. All the smiles on people's faces whenever they tried my brand. The moment I no longer felt invisible and people saw me.

I found that when I started giving myself new experiences it made a huge impact. Despite my negative self-doubt and obstacles, I was persevering!

Create new experiences and stretch yourself. Whether it's taking that step to start a business, taking on more challenges at work, pitching an idea, going back to school, creating a mom's group, or applying for that exciting position you only dreamed of.

Whatever it is that *you* dream of—that is what life is about. New experiences that will change your beliefs, definitions, and perspective. In each change, new life lives.

What if you asked your boss for that new position?

What if you applied for that Small Business loan?

What if you went back to school to get your MBA?

What dreams are you following or want to follow?

Year after year, while I was growing my brand, I would tell my story. I would be driven to keep going by the idea that if I reached tremendous success, then I can inspire other women to have the courage to start their own business. In my mind, even after growing the business to a multi-million-dollar brand, I still didn't feel like I made it. I've since learned that it's not about "making it." It's about the journey and all the experiences each step of the way. And the more I told my story, the more women wanted to know. Enjoy the road that leads to your dreams. Take time to stop and look at the scenery.

You'll rarely regret the things you do but will regret the things you don't do. So, if you're not developing yourself to achieve your dream, then you're just a dreamer. It's not only your responsibly to make your dream happen for you, but the world is waiting for you to show up. No one will ever be as passionate about your dream as you are. Today is the day for no excuses.

Let faith empower you and take the risk. Don't just be a dreamer, be a doer. "Your dream" could change someone's life or even the world. There is so much power in your story, your dream. Speak up, speak out, speak often—and share your dream with us. We need it and we need *you*.

If I can do it—you certainly can too!

A few of my favorite tips to help you persevere and dream big…

1. Is your dream worth staying up all hours of the night? Is it worth spending a Saturday night working towards it instead of lying on the couch binging on Netflix? Is your dream worth the risk of failure? Make sure your dream is worth sacrificing things in your life.

2. Have a clear vision of your dreams and what your goals are. Write them down. Define them; be specific. Spend time visualizing the life you wish to create. If someone asked you your dreams, would you be able to describe them succinctly? You'll be able to take own your dreams and be proud of them only when you truly understand what they are.

3. Make *every* minute of *every* day count towards your goals and dreams. Don't live the life others expect of you and follow your heart. It's a slow process but remember quitting won't speed it up. And on days when you just can't believe in yourself, reach out to someone who does believe in you. This really helps!

Glow Girl Affirmation:
My potential to succeed is limitless.

6

Spark Change

"I do not wish women to have power over men; but over themselves."

—*Mary Shelley*

UNFORTUNATELY, IT IS still our reality as women to face workplace challenges like lack of respect, sexual harassment, and manterruptions (not letting us speak) simply because we are women. And if you work in a male dominated industry all the above can be magnified.

How many of you have wondered how to get to the top of your company? How many of you are trying to build a business in a male dominated field? We are working hard battling our way into corporate positions or male dominated industries and are still getting passed over for promotions and not being given the respect we deserve.

I've experienced this first hand being in a male dominated field for nearly a decade. It's mind-boggling to me how so many assumptions are made just merely because of gender. How I felt I had to prove myself to the men in my industry—mostly investors. It's not bad enough that I work so hard every day to prove to *myself* that I can build a successful company, I also have to prove my worth and abilities to my male counterparts.

I had to show up to board meetings with a game face on and continually prove that I deserved to be there, whereas respect is inherently earned by the males. I can't even begin to count the number of times I've been called "darling" and "honey," or been treated like I'm not in a leadership role.

The truth is, women are thought leaders and contribute a unique set of skills and creative ideas that can exponentially help a company's strategies and growth.

A few years ago, I was at a conference and the badges we were given had only our name and our company name. On the first night there was a networking event and it was mostly men. As I was meeting people, one by one each guy would ask what I do for my beverage company with a question and an assumed position. I would hear, "So, what do you do for Sipp...marketing?" or "So, what do you do for Sipp...sales?" They wouldn't even let me answer. Every question I got like that I answered, "yes." I did do marketing and sales among many other things like finance, production, formulations, logistics, customer service, and running the company.

The following day, I was scheduled to present on stage and all those guys who assumed what I did and never assumed I was the CEO or founder found out what I really did. After I spoke, many of them came up to me and said, "Wow, how come you didn't tell me you are the founder and CEO of Sipp?" I responded with, "How come you assumed I wasn't." Boom. Mic drop.

The biggest challenge is perhaps the "bro-club" mentality. It's one thing to say that there is a glass ceiling for women, but it's an added challenge when you are not part of the "club" because you're a woman.

There are so many preconceived notions about women in business. Like the way we dress or how we react. If a woman is wearing a short skirt, she may be considered not very smart or not to be taken seriously. If a woman is too emotional then she must be "on her period." And if we dare to speak out, then we are a bitch.

I was actually told by an investor that because I'm creative I can't be successful in growing a large business. Really? Who says? Why can't I be both? Because I'm a woman?

How anyone sees you has nothing to do with your worthiness. Never be diminished by the opinions of *anyone* no matter what their position is or how important they think they are.

As you probably know by now, I always try to find the positive in everything. While this is real and women have to deal with it every day, I don't want us to fall victim to it. We are much stronger than that. We can choose to complain or take action.

So, what are the things that might hold us back that we *can* control?

Don't be afraid to fail. As women we tend to fear that mistakes in the workplace or business could cost us our job or success. Failure is all part of the journey and brings you closer to figuring things out. #failforward

Having a family can make us look like we are not career driven and not dedicated since we are balancing a job or running a company and also being a mom. We also can feel inferior by believing things we have been told when we were younger. Women are meant to be in the home while the man is the bread winner. Men are better equipped to be strong leaders and achieve success.

My philosophy is be yourself. I see many women who feel like they have to act like a man to get ahead or get things accomplished. I've seen women not talk about their family because it might make them look not focused or driven. I've seen women hide their compassionate side to make then appear stronger. I'm guilty of some of these things as I was trying to prove myself. Don't cave in. Be strong in your own way. Be honest, talk about your kids, develop deep relationships with your customers or clients. Be open and transparent and do your thing!

We need to lead like the strong ladies we are and when we break through the barriers one by one it will propel us forward.

It seems we need to work so much harder than men just to prove ourselves to be equal and I was determined to show my investors what a woman could do and open their minds.

When I would attempt to justify my worth crediting myself for the creation of unique original flavors, my work ethic, traveling three to four times a month sacrificing time away from my son, building an extremely dedicated team, selling into large retail chains we only dreamed of getting in; I was still told that money is more valuable than that. What? Someone could have a boatload of money but without a great idea, a story, and lots of hard what do you have? The same boatload of money and no way to grow it.

I hustled like nobody's business and could have killed myself trying to prove my worth and value to them. They still didn't see it. Insensitive men will break you down and I was made to feel "less than" by intimidating tactics. Their sexist attitudes only added fuel to the insecurities I was already battling.

As I entered my teen years, my stepfather's verbal abuse and dismissiveness began to overlap with my dad's newfound controlling ways. I wanted to work as soon as I could, and I got an early work permit and started working at the age of fifteen. I had to be driven to work so after I turned sixteen, my dad decided to give me a used car to go back and forth to work. Only work. No driving it to school, no going to the store or McDonald's down the street from me or anywhere but work. I begged to drive it just to a friend's house in the same town. It was an emphatic *no*.

Because I didn't live with my dad and just saw him on the weekends, after having the car for a few months, I decided to take a chance and drive to my friend's house after work one day. Then became braver and drove it to school one day that same week. At the end of that week, I drove to my dad's house to stay for the weekend. Shortly after I arrived, he went out to the garage which he would often do to tinker when suddenly I heard a loud voice shouting from outside. I ran to the door thinking something happened to him and there he was standing in the driveway angrily waving his hand and motioning for me to come out.

His face was flush, and he had the scariest look on his face. I had seen this occasionally before and was petrified. I felt like I couldn't breathe. I opened the front door and descended the cement steps having no idea what he was about to say. I was filled with anxiety. *What could I have possibly done wrong to make him this angry?* I thought.

He asked me if I drove the car more than just to work that past week. My mouth was so dry I felt like I couldn't speak. With a very shaky voice, I said, "No...well...um...actually one day after work I went to my friend Abby's house." I nervously continued, "Um...she lives super close by and needed some notes I had for class the next day." I saw his face become redder and he unleashed. He said he knew that I didn't just go to Abby's house and said I was lying and demanded me to tell him the entire truth.

I knew it was only going to get worse. At the same time, I couldn't figure out how he knew, I mean this was the 80s! No tracking technology existed. He motioned for me to come into the garage and I dutifully followed. And there on a metal pole in the center of the garage was a clipboard dangling on a nail. A clipboard of "death." That's how I felt—dead.

It was my dad's way of tracking all my miles and unbeknownst to me, he had been keeping track of my miles every week and matched it with my work schedule to know the exact miles that should be on my car upon his "weekly inspection." I was in shock and I felt sick. I couldn't believe that my dad was doing this.

He reprimanded me and I felt like I had to leave and go

back home. I couldn't handle how upset he was with me. I was crying and I ran inside to get my things and he asked where I was going, and I was sobbing so hard at that point that I couldn't speak. He said sternly, "You can't drive in your condition!" Still so upset, I got in my car and was ready to escape. My dad's driveway was on an angle and I was never the best at backing up, but with tear filled eyes, I ended up going up on his grass trying to back out of the driveway. *Ugh!* I thought. *Seriously, could this possibly get any worse?* I tried not to look as I was leaving, but out of the corner of my eye, I saw him angrily pointing at the lawn I just left tires tracks in.

Over time, he eased up some. I know he was worried something might happen to me and he struggled with letting me go. But this was such a pivotal day in my life. Life changing. I felt small. I felt scared. I felt intimidated. I felt stupid. I felt it was my fault.

Daughters often view their self-worth through their father's eyes and draw strength from their acceptance, encouragement, and pride. Love and acceptance from my dad meant the world to me. Fathers set the course for their daughter's life.

In *A Woman's Worth*, Marianne Williamson says, "The story doesn't begin with grown women being massacred in the workplace or in the press. It begins with innocent little girls who become convinced, for whatever reason, that the girl within them isn't good enough."

I learned my value was dependent on my actions. As I got older, I continued to suffer from low self-esteem and was vastly intimidated by men. Even so, I had a feeling inside me that I wanted to do something big. Despite my low self-esteem and shyness, I felt destined to create and grow. I didn't know how, but I was driven. I eventually learned I didn't need to be perfect, I just needed to be myself. And I was enough.

Your value doesn't decrease based on a man's inability to see your worth.

This is our story, not just mine, and it's time for us to spark change. It's the countless times we've been called "sweetie," or heard "it must be hormones," or the idea we worked on so hard is called "cute" or the all the times we didn't get the chance to move ahead or be a part of something or get that raise because a man did. We can be creative, and we can be a CEO, and we can be a success.

Hell... we need to be the CEO our parents hoped we would marry!

When I took a corporate job in my twenties, I had a boss who I considered the devil. Seriously, he wore all black all day every day.

If you were late for the morning team meeting he would lock the door to the conference room and you had to stand outside until they were done and then when "the almighty" emerged you had to follow him to his office, close the door, and explain why you were late. And as I'm sure you guess there were no morning meeting donuts. After he grilled you with twenty questions while popping anti-acids and chugging down his black coffee, he would finally dismiss you with a harsh warning. I was only late once. Once was enough.

I witnessed co-workers leaving his office in tears on a weekly basis. I witnessed him flicking a cigarette butt at someone and one of my co-workers left her cubicle one afternoon after meeting with him. And it wasn't just for the day. She left her cubicle with everything in it, including framed family photos, and never returned. I did everything I could to stay on his good side. Until, the day I was supposed to receive a bonus and I didn't get it.

I asked to meet with him so I could figure out what happened. I had no idea what was in store for me. I simply asked him if he could check and see why I didn't receive my bonus. He reacted with a very baffled look. Then questioned me, "why would you expect to receive your bonus now?" I replied, "because I earned it." He said, "you earn it when I say you earn it."

I was extremely confused because I didn't understand why he would be holding onto *my* bonus. He informed me that the protocol is to come and ask him for it and he will decide when I get it. Seriously, *ask him for it?* I began to see that this was his way of controlling me. Of keeping me under his thumb. I explained to him that I needed the bonus for a down payment. As I was sitting there, I had the realization, *why do I feel like I need to explain what I'm going to use my bonus for? It was none of his business.* Then he actually asked me how much of my bonus did I need. He said he would be willing to give me a portion of it to "hold me over."

When I stood up for myself and said that I was due my entire bonus, he abruptly jumped up from his chair and leaned over his desk with his eyes bulging out of his head (and he had a big head) and began to yell loudly in my face saying, "who do you think you are asking for your full bonus? This man more than six feet tall dressed all in black was hovering over me and screaming in my face as spit was projecting across the desk right towards me.

I immediately cowered and was fearful. I felt tears welling up in my eyes and I was praying that I wasn't going to cry. At that point as he continued berating me; I had no control. Once he noticed a tear streaming down my cheek he stopped and looked at me with disgust, shaking his head. He then said, "wow you're really going to cry now? Some man must've really done a number on you in your past...that's all I can say." He abruptly dismissed me.

I could not believe that those words came out of his mouth. Putting aside the barrage of statements he previously said including calling me "stupid," this took the cake. This comment cut me to the core and was so disturbing. I had to leave his office immediately and the following day I met with the CEO of the company and asked to be transferred to another division effective immediately. I was one of his top performers and my boss was not happy.

While I felt proud of myself that I stood up and made this request, the impression that it gave to my boss and the CEO of the company was that *I* couldn't handle *him*. So, it was me that was the problem. Never was it positioned as his behavior was completely unacceptable. And while I was most likely triggered from my past, that's not relevant. *No one* should have to endure this type of behavior, no matter who you are or what you've gone through.

But because of what he said, that comment stuck with me for a long time with a small part of me believing that he was right, and I overreacted because I was damaged. Now I emphatically know that is not true. No one deserves that. This is where the shift needs to happen. *We* need to be the ones to make the change.

When I heard this quote from Michelle Obama it hit me to the core: "Women, we endure those cuts in so many ways that we don't even notice we're cut. We are living with small tiny cuts, and we are bleeding every single day. And we're still getting up."

How often do you think or feel something but you're afraid to speak up? As women, sometimes we feel we should just agree with everything or everyone. I mean it's the reasonable thing to do. And who wants to rock the boat and possibly deal with confrontation?

If we want to have a voice, we need to speak up and that might come with some confrontation. It's always harder to speak your mind and stand for something. But it's our time.

Own your voice. Speak with authority and don't undermine yourself by starting with, "I'm not sure, but…" or even worse don't start with an apology. When you start a sentence with

"I'm sorry, but I think we should…," you lose all impact in the point you want to make or the idea you want to share.

Be brave. Women should not have to feel intimated to speak their minds and share their ideas.

Faith over fear, sister!

Be confident. Don't second-guess yourself. If you don't believe in yourself, then it's going to be nearly impossible to make others believe in you too, especially in a male-dominated industry.

Powerful quote from Audre Lorde: "Next time, ask: what's the worst that will happen? Then push yourself a little further than you dare. Once you start to speak, people will yell at you. They will interrupt you, put you down, and suggest it's personal. And the world won't end…And the speaking will get easier and easier. And you will find you have fallen in love with your own vision, which you may never have realized you had. And you will lose some friends and lovers and realize you don't miss them. And new ones will find you and cherish you…And at last you'll know with surpassing certainty that only one thing is more frightening than speaking your truth. And that is not speaking."

Be prepared for rejection when you refuse to be manipulated.

I was essentially pushed out of my own company that I created. Was it because I am a woman? I believe so. And because I'm a woman, I was different. Different than what they were used to, especially as I became stronger. And when I really began to speak my mind, they didn't like it. I challenged ideas (it was my creation—it came from my brain). I stood for the integrity of my brand and my story, but in the end, it was apparently time for me to move on. We didn't value things in the same way.

The conversations that were had without my knowledge just prior to my departure, I will never know. I was purpose-fully left out. And not only by my investors, but someone I completely trusted who worked right alongside me. Someone who *I* hired and trusted to be a part of the company *I* created. Someone who I was paying a decent salary to and could support his family. Someone who repeatedly said, "I have your back." Someone who restored my faith in men in business. Someone who I completely trusted. This someone stabbed me in my back. This someone betrayed me and shook me to the core.

The saddest thing about betrayal is that it never comes from your enemies.

So many men over the years told me that they "have my back" and ultimately ended up stabbing me in the back. Make sure that everyone who's in your "boat" is rowing and not drilling holes behind you when you're not looking.

It's taken me some time to bounce back from how everything played out but, I finally woke up one day and realized he doesn't deserve one more minute of time in my thoughts. The one thing I know, is that nothing will cease to amaze me in business now. That's what he taught me. And even though his betrayal could make me bitter or shut me down and scare me to open up and be vulnerable again, I refuse to give him that power. I decided to turn distrust into determination. I stand strong with integrity and dignity.

Don't let people like this rent space in your head. Raise the rent and evict them! *Bye*!

This quote really resonated with me from Steve Maraboli: "I am grateful to those who have betrayed me... They thought they were just stabbing me in the back, but they were also cutting me free from their poisonous life."

Remember, whoever is trying to bring you down is already beneath you.

I've since learned that female CEOs are much more likely to be dismissed by investors from their own company than male CEOs. And when a female CEO is terminated, she's usually replaced by a man. And it's ironic because there's been research done that shows a company that has more gender balance in leadership roles, are in fact more profitable.

Love this Mexican proverb: "They tried to bury us; they did not know we were the seeds."

I am now finally stepping out from under the black cloud of scrutiny I was under and speaking my mind and it's a freeing and powerful feeling. I'm shining a light on it and growing.

If you are a CEO or founder of your own business, value yourself equitably. We need to be the game changers. We need to ensure equal pay. When women running their own companies set higher salaries for themselves, it sends a clear message of what they're worth, to investors and themselves.

Not only have I spoken to many women entrepreneurs about this, but I was in this situation myself. My investors didn't value me and therefore only paid me far less than what they paid a man in my exact position. And when I brought up a raise, I was made to be felt like how dare I even ask for something comparable. They continued to push me down and it's a disgrace—we need to rise up.

Everything that forced me down, showed me the power to rise.

The reality is that we have to do double the work in order to succeed and prove ourselves, with less pay. It's just like what they said about the infamous Ginger Rogers: she did everything Fred Astaire did, except backwards and in high heels.

We may not be able to change the perception of men in our industry, but we can change our outlook. Look at it as a source of motivation for change. We need to glow together!

Women are great at building relationships, empowering others, understanding people, and multi-tasking—skills that are great assets, not liabilities, in the workplace or building a business.

These are our weapons and that's how I grew my female-centric business.

Now it's time we lean in, lean out, stand tall, and move forward in the shoes of our choice!

My mission is to empower women to spark change and not just sit back and wait for the change to happen. It's up to us to make the change.

We should not be waiting around for someone to empower us. We need to empower ourselves.

Let's pave the path for the women coming up behind us. #womenempoweringwomen

While I may be fighting the fight in a man's world, I am reminded I am a woman.

A phenomenal woman. Thank you, Maya Angelou for this poem:

Phenomenal Woman.

It's the fire in my eyes,

And the flash of my teeth,

The swing in my waist,

And the joy in my feet.

I'm a woman

Phenomenally.

Phenomenal woman,

That's me.

Those who throw stones in your path give you materials for the foundation of your character. Now I'm rebuilding even stronger.

Looking back, I know I was put through trials and tribulations, but they all taught me something.

All the obstacles I had to overcome made me stronger, wiser, and helped me achieve who and what I am today. And now I'm here to empower other women.

As strong women, we don't need to be like a man. We need

to celebrate what makes us unique, embrace our assets, and shine. You glow girl!

A few of my favorite tips to help you spark change...

1. Did you know that women founders received only 2.2% of all venture capital dollars in 2018? If you are trying to raise money to start or grow your business I would start with friends and family, angel investors, or I highly recommend crowdfunding like Kickstarter, Indiegogo, or women-centric iFundWomen. If you need to go the path of venture capital and they *say* they invest in people first and that people are most important, my word of advice is to ask to speak with references.

2. Be fearless with passion. Whether you want to go after that dream job or start a new business you need courage and passion. Take risks, go beyond what you can think of, and venture into unknown territories. Do not shy away from trying something new and always be fearless when you are following your passion. The biggest risk is you take is not taking one at all.

3. Don't be overly apologetic and speak up when you have something valuable to contribute. And don't let anyone else's opinion of you become your opinion of you. Take credit for your good ideas and hard work and put yourself forward for tasks. Make yourself known and own it!

Glow Girl Affirmation:
I am worthy of respect
and acceptance.

7

The Therapist

"And then the day came when the risk to remain in a tight bud was more painful than the risk it took to blossom."

—*Anais Nin*

THERAPIST, AKA LIFESAVER. I feel extremely fortunate that when I felt like I was drowning I had the courage to continue swimming with the help of, you guessed it, a therapist.

Some people are under the impression that therapy is for wimps. This couldn't be further from the truth. It's exactly the opposite. It takes strength and courage to decide to see a therapist. I can speak for myself and it was by far one of the best decisions I ever made.

Therapy can be talking to a friend, a family member, a loved one, a women's group, a box of dark chocolates, or a pastor and while these are great options (especially the chocolate); speaking to a trained therapist offers benefits beyond simply being a good listener.

There was a saying I recently heard, *don't ask someone for directions how to get somewhere that they've never been.* This is so true! How many times have you had someone trying to give you unsolicited advice that has never even experienced what you're going through? A professional, even if they haven't been through what you've been through has been trained to listen, ask questions, and to give advice only when appropriate (the best ones hardly ever give advice).

Often times we downplay our challenges and tell ourselves we can handle this on our own. We don't want to appear being weak and I think as women we tend to think we can handle it all. After all, we are master multi-taskers!

To rise to your best self, you have to be vulnerable and willing to change. To change your life, you need to invest in your self-love journey. While you may feel compelled to fix things on your own, you might not be able to see what someone else can. We are so close to the problem or issue that it's difficult to see it from different angles. Perspective is a gift but often we need assistance in attaining it.

You may also think your problems are too trivial so you shouldn't go. Trust me, I felt that way for the first six months of therapy and can you believe I would ask my therapist at the end of the session, "Are you sure my problems are serious enough to come here?" My self-esteem was so low that I thought I was taking away time from someone who truly needed his help. Thank God, he reassured me I was just as important as anyone else and I was able to get past that. Don't feel guilty about talking to a therapist and taking their time. No one has ever faced the (exact) challenges that you have, and you will never face the exact challenges of someone else. All we have is our experience living the life we were given, therefore any obstacles that come your way—whether they're as big as a supernova or as small as an atom—are valid. You deserve to receive help no matter what.

It's so important to look at where you came from to know where you're going. It's not easy to look at all the difficult stuff you've gone through. Sometimes it feels so much easier to stay right where you are. We as human beings always gravitate toward (perceived) comfort and away from the "unknown," even if that unknown is better for you than staying where you are. You may think, *why would I want to relive that pain again?* Especially if you have to face some tough things from your past. But trust me when I say, sister, it's worth it.

And knowing yourself is better than not knowing.

Aristotle once said, "Knowing yourself is the beginning of all wisdom."

Therapy can help you learn things about yourself you might not have figured out on your own and break lifelong patterns such as negative self-talk, low self-esteem, trauma, or grief and guide you on a journey to your greatness.

My life in therapy has been a life-changing transformational journey.

Discovering things about yourself can be painful. I uncovered many things about myself through therapy and even the process of writing this book that were extremely emotional. That being said, strange and wonderful things may begin to happen as you do the work to forgive, heal, and learn to love yourself—first.

You gain resilience and insight. You begin to see who you are and how to love yourself.

I feel like therapy took me from lost to found. Some people spend their entire lives unaware of who they are. When you are in a therapist's office there is no place to hide.

There were so many times in my childhood when I felt like I wanted to hide. I didn't feel good about myself and the turmoil in my home life was taking a toll on me.

When I was about ten-years-old, Sundays became one of the worst nights for me. The positive was that I saw my dad every weekend after my parents' divorce, but the negative was coming back home on Sunday nights. I hated knowing my dad was going to be alone after he dropped me off. Tears followed Sunday after Sunday.

I continued to feel so bad, I began to call my dad every Sunday night. I needed to make sure he was okay. Why did *I* feel responsible for *his* happiness? I was just a child.

Think about the things that you felt responsible for that shouldn't have been. What are you still holding on to? We need to release the burdens that were never ours to carry in the first place.

My dad would usually take me to do something fun on the weekends and occasionally he would buy me something. Despite having to leave him Sunday night I would at least be excited to come home and share the details of my weekend, but I quickly learned that wasn't allowed. If my stepfather saw me come in with a bag, he would tell me to go immediately upstairs and put it in my bedroom closet and he didn't want me talking about my "great time" with anyone.

This made me want to hide and I would retreat in my room in tears. I wanted to share the joy of my weekend, but instead I felt shame.

When we are little we are naturally filled with light and exuberance. If we are met with messages like the one I received from my stepfather to "be quiet," it makes us shrink and feel small. It made me feel disconnected, unimportant, and invisible.

Are you ready to come out of hiding?

Are you ready to become the best version of yourself?

Are you ready to evolve?

We are all human and we can all use some help. It's nothing to be ashamed of. You need to find the right vehicle to get you where you want to go. We all have things happening in our lives so whether we have a specific problem or not, it's always good to talk. Think about all you've gone through in your life and I'm sure you've had some challenges that were probably not easy to manage or control.

Do you still think about them often? If so, they are most likely unresolved and may be holding you back in some way, and you might not even know it. Address any past issues that pop up so you can work through them. Trust me, if you don't, they will keep hanging around until you do.

Lessons in life will be repeated until they are learned.

I decided to talk to a therapist and see if it would help with issues from my marriage, my dad, and my business. I wanted to be truly happy and have peace in my life. Little did I know what would be uncovered. I had so many unresolved issues buried so deep I didn't know they were there.

I was running a successful business, so I told myself I must be okay. But week after week, these deep layers were being discovered. It was scary how much I swept under the carpet just to function. It was like opening Pandora's box.

Sometimes you have to go through the darkness to get to the light.

It's funny because when I decided to seek help, I searched for a female therapist. I thought I would feel more comfortable since I've had some "issues" with men in my life. I left a message for a woman therapist and I got a call back from a man. He said his name was Todd and he asked if I wanted to come in and meet with him to see if it would be a fit for what I was looking to accomplish. I agreed and it was the best decision I made.

From that first meeting, I felt confident Todd was the one to help me. He understood me. He heard me. He "saw" me. I was no longer invisible. He was guiding me, encouraging me, and lifting me up so my light could shine brightly.

The connection you have with your therapist is essential. You need someone who you can trust—someone you feel comfortable talking to about difficult issues and intimate secrets, someone who you feel safe with. Someone you trust. This is critical for success

The key is to find a therapist who listens well, empathizes, and empowers you with the bravery and perseverance to tackle the work ahead. And if you don't vibe with your therapist (with few exceptions it's good to try them out for at least four sessions) then you can always search for another. If you didn't like your child's pediatrician, you wouldn't give up because "pediatrics doesn't work" and "all pediatricians are bad." You would keep searching for a great pediatrician until you found one you like. We need to treat our mental health the same as we would our physical health; and truly it's not much different; it's all "health."

I needed help to forge through many obstacles facing me in my life and the inner-child was in there feeling pretty scared, but I knew I was finally ready to invest the time in me and do the necessary work. My new mantra was, "I am woman hear me roar!" (Compliments of Todd.) He said that he would help me work toward becoming my best self and I felt in my heart he could.

Have you ever noticed how tumbling a problem around and around in your head often gets you nowhere? What I experienced in therapy was being shown something in an entirely different way. Not complex—incredibly simple, but different from what I was used to doing. It's a mind shift and there are circumstances in our life that we can't see any other way on our own no matter how we try.

When my therapist presents something differently that I've been struggling with, it's like a light bulb goes off above my head (I call them Toddisms!). *How does that happen?* I think. *I'm smart. How did I never see it that way?* Again, we are so close to the situation often it's hard to see past it. Every time I saw something from a different perspective, I would write it down in my journal and I began slowly chugging along, learning, and growing step by step.

The more I was learning in therapy, the more I wanted to know. I read books, researched, did a lot of self-talk and journaling. I could feel the change and I knew I was growing. And when I doubted it on those challenging days (and, girl, you know we all have them) I would look back in my journal and see where I was at even three months prior and it made it clear. You can't challenge something that is staring you in the face in black and white. That's the deep impact of journaling.

I learned so many things over the past six years once I decided to take charge of my life. I'm still learning on my journey and it's so exciting to imagine where I will be in the next six years. There is such power in knowing you are in control. If you have the tools and the knowledge, it's up to you to apply them.

I truly didn't even see at the time that life could be any different than it was. It was all I knew.

Just think about that for a moment. If you are feeling like you are stuck, depressed, or in a place that you can't see the light at the end of the tunnel, just take that first baby step and make a connection. Baby steps are still moving forward.

Many of us grew up under the impression that emotional feelings shouldn't be discussed. This is the worst thing you can do for yourself. Stuffing your emotions down and not working through issues, especially if there was any serious abuse or trauma in the past, can create a myriad of problems later on in life.

I struggled with low self-esteem and Todd knew just the right things to say to lift me up. For me, this was critical. This was needed because I was at another low point in my life when my flame was barely lit. I had difficulty building myself up. I knew how, but at this stage of my life I was so low my "go to" tools were not strong enough. I needed someone like him to point out how strong and resilient I was. And because he was a professional, I believed him. I trusted he knew what he was talking about and I listened.

While I believe the most important relationship we can

have is with ourselves and we are responsible for our own happiness, sometimes we need some help and that's okay. A president needs a cabinet and a CEO needs a board of directors. I remember times he would point out one of my positive traits or abilities and when he would utter the words, they sounded so foreign to me. But word after word I took it in, journaled about it, repeated it to myself, and eventually began to see it for myself. He was building me back up again, word by word.

It's about progress, not perfection.

Imagine talking with someone who wants to get to know you, not to judge you or have expectations or demands. Someone who wants to learn about your past to understand how you need to be accepted. Someone to help you to find new skills and tools to deal with challenges and different ways to look at situations in your life.

Every time I entered Todd's office; I took a deep breath. I could let my guard down and just be myself. I was safe. I could be vulnerable. I cried. I let go.

Just imagine that feeling. Being fully open to embrace what your life could truly become.

I worked hard and every step of the way he let me know how well I was doing. I was feeling proud of my accomplishments and facing my fears. He said he believed in me and my success and when I doubted it, he would look right at me and emphatically say, "I know you will be a success." I asked him, "how can this messed up girl be the one who makes it?" With an emotional pause he said, "because you will truly help people with your story." He saw that in me before I saw it in myself.

After my first few months of going to therapy, my friends saw a huge difference in me. My confidence was higher; I felt more powerful week by week and most importantly, I was feeling happier.

Do you feel like some days you wake up and you think, *this going to be an awesome day?* And then, boom, you get hit with a curve ball. Instead of possibly spiraling out of control we can learn how to handle these curve balls in a healthier way. What a difference it makes when you can effectively handle unexpected challenges one after the other. Hey, baseball players get training on how to deal with unexpected curve balls so why shouldn't we?

You don't have to struggle through life with low self-esteem or low confidence. Don't be paralyzed by it and sister, please give yourself the opportunity to explore your past. I learned that uncovering these "parts" of me who were keeping me down and creating self-doubt was so critical to improving my self-esteem. Acknowledging where they are coming from helps to address them when they come up.

Going to therapy is a process so it will require some patience. When I felt stuck and I began to get impatient it always seemed to be right before a breakthrough or "aha moment," and in therapy I've had many. It's such a rewarding feeling knowing I could have just given up and walked away out of frustration but when you stick it out you could discover something about yourself that could be life-changing. Your perspective changes and your sense of possibility expands further than you imagined. It's truly the best feeling and every time that happens, I feel my light glow even brighter.

It's so easy to feel overwhelmed by a problem when it's this big swirling massive cloud hanging over your head. Talking it through piece by piece is so helpful to break up the cloud and things are bound to come out when you engage. Then you feel clearer and can look at it in a more logical way and to know what direction you want to go in or how to manage it.

I didn't just "go" to therapy. I studied what my therapist told me, I journaled about it, and I used the tools over and over. Awareness is not enough—I had to take action.

I believe that journaling is the entryway to our soul. When you were younger, did you ever have a diary? If so, do you remember how you felt writing in it? I distinctly remember mine was pink, with a Holly Hobbie print on the front cover and a tiny padlock and an even tinier key. I would write my innermost thoughts (aka—boy crushes) and lots of heart doodles always starting with, "Dear Diary." After I poured my heart out, they would then be locked away for safe keeping. I loved my diary but as I got older, I never seemed to make the time to write. I was just living, experiencing life, while Holly Hobbie became a distant memory.

After going to therapy and with all that life was throwing at me, I decided to give journaling a whirl again. It was life-changing. It calls a wandering mind to attention. It creates mindfulness.

You can create your own personal blueprint to build the life you want. You wouldn't build a house without a blueprint, right? So why not have a blueprint for your life? Journal about your dreams and goals. Get specific.

Continually writing them down increases the likelihood of achieving them. Writing them has the power to make them become a reality. I am living proof of this.

Journaling is an outlet for processing emotions and increases self-awareness.

You'll find that after you poured your innermost feelings on paper (or on your computer or phone or with your chisel and stone tablet), there is a freeing sense of release. Instead of this swirling mass of thoughts and feelings you feel a sense of calmness and clarity.

The emotional release from journaling lowers anxiety, stress, and induces better sleep.

It declutters your brain. It can help you make rational decisions.

Journaling is one of the most important things to do in your life. If done effectively, it can change *everything* in your life for the better.

You'll become the person you want to be.

You'll design the life you want to live.

Your relationships will be healthier and happier.

You'll be more productive and powerful.

You will feel gratitude.

There's a lot of power in the written word. It's helped me through loss, grief, working through big decisions, documenting life changing experiences, and expressing my innermost thoughts, dreams, and goals.

Just like the power of positive thinking, there's the power of positive writing. If you're already journaling, good for you! If not, I encourage you to start off simple by writing 2-3 things that you're grateful for and 2-3 things you would like to accomplish each day and see what gems of wisdom and positivity emerge.

It's fascinating to go back a year or two and see how far you've progressed. In our day-to-day life we may not see how far we've come. Once you see it in writing you acknowledge your growth and it will fuel you to keep going. When I reflect back, I'm amazed that the exact goals I wrote for myself, I accomplished or am now working towards.

Here is one of my journal entries from July 2013:

Today I'm trying to realize that I am an inspiration. This is hard when I really think about why I can't except this of myself. I think about how even to this day both my parents are not happy about my choice of building my beverage business (which I know mostly is because they see how hard I'm working and a job would be easier) but I think if it were my child I would be so proud and happy for her that she's following her passion. How often do people find their passion? This brings me back to why I am doing this. I believe it's to help others find and follow their passion and to not let others stop you with their doubts or negativity. It's hard to have faith in yourself, but if you just take the first step, God puts people around you that help give you the faith and give you the confidence to take the next step. As you take each step you start building the confidence on your own to keep moving forward. Taking time to reflect helps too - realizing and acknowledging that "I did this!" Those negative thoughts start to chip away.

Talking with Todd today I realized when someone says to me, "you are an inspiration" I think my "actions" inspire people but not "me" - the core of who I am. It's who I am acting like. That makes me sad that I can't acknowledge that. I know I will get there. Persistence and patience. Since I keep all my personal struggles hidden in my business life, I feel like two different people inside one person. My therapist said if people are inspired by me when they don't even know all of my past and my inner struggles, imagine how they would feel if they did know and how inspirational that would be once I share my story. He seems to always put things into perspective and all in a way I can understand and truly makes me feel better and stronger in my core being. Thank you, Todd.

Takeaways from today's session (Toddisms): I need to keep moving forward! What is the best predictor of the future? The past! And I have never given up. I am a fighter — even in my marriage. I've done everything in my power to save my marriage. I fought and persevered to grow my business and I am now taking time to focus on my personal growth.

Going back in my journal allows me to not only see the progress, but also what my aspirations were at that time.

You get in life what you have the courage to ask for.

As women, we have the tendency to be caregivers and then end up putting ourselves on the backburner. You don't even know how you truly feel because you are so tired or stressed out. You don't have or make the time to take care of the most important person in the world—you.

Do you feel overwhelmed, like you are at the end of your rope? Are you trying to just survive getting through each day feeling like there's no hope for a better, brighter future?

My hope for you is that you feel confident enough to cope with life's challenges and disappointments and to know that you deserve to experience love and acceptance from others as well as from yourself.

Show up for yourself.

Show yourself some grace and care. Show yourself love. Take some time to reflect and put away all the ideas of what you "should be." Invest in yourself.

You are worthy.

Embrace yourself for who you are and where you are. Stop playing small. Quit putting yourself last. Stop apologizing and know and appreciate that you are here despite any setbacks or negative experiences you have had.

When you make the decision that you want better for yourself everything shifts.

I once heard an analogy about a cocoon and the butterfly and how through therapy we can become a beautiful butterfly. I thought about this further and how the caterpillar crawls into the cocoon and liquifies. When we enter therapy, we don't know what's going to happen. We have to "break down our parts" like the caterpillar. It could be dark and scary, and dealing with our emotions can make it feel like it gets worse before it gets better (hang in there, sister); but like the butterfly, beautiful wings await us. If the caterpillars knew what was waiting for them in the cocoon, do you think there would be any butterflies?

I feel like a butterfly now and it was not an easy transformation. I think I must have been stuck in the cocoon for a decade. It doesn't matter how long you are in the cocoon as long as you are "breaking down your parts." I know for a fact, if it weren't for my therapist I would not be where I am today. I can't even begin to imagine where I might be without therapy. I am continually telling him how he changed my life and he reminds me that I was the one that did all the work (#truth). I can only hope that by me living my purpose to inspire, guide, and uplift that I can make the kind of difference in other's lives that has been made in mine.

It's about the journey, not the destination. There's no timeline on healing.

Growth is difficult and everyone wants a quick fix, but it takes time. Be patient with yourself; don't get discouraged with setbacks and celebrate positive changes in your life.

What's the alternative?

I am here to validate you, to encourage you to conquer your past. Allow yourself to be open and to be seen. Be vulnerable. It can be life changing if you let it. It may be scary at first, but the risk is so worth the reward.

Owning your story and loving yourself with grace through the therapy process is the bravest and most deeply loving thing you can do.

This is one of my absolute favorite quotes from Brené Brown: "Owning our story can be hard but not nearly as difficult as spending our lives running from it. Embracing our vulnerabilities is risky but not nearly as dangerous as giving up on love and belonging and joy—the experiences that make us the most vulnerable. Only when we are brave enough to explore the darkness will we discover the infinite power of our light."

You have everything inside you to conquer your past and live the life you deserve. No matter how broken or damaged you may feel you have everything inside you to be complete, happy, and fulfilled—but you need someone to help facilitate that process.

And one last word before I get off of my soapbox: Tell your story. Speak up, speak out, speak often. Start in a small, safe place but let it grow little by little in whatever direction it takes you. Define yourself before others do. Owning your story can change and save your life; but it also has such incredible power to change and save other's lives as well. It doesn't matter how old, young, gay, disabled or able bodied, brown, or anything else; whatever and whoever you are—you need you and *we* need you!

A few of my favorite tips to help you reclaim yourself through therapy…

1. The first step is to decide you want help. You are ready to take off your mask and come out of hiding. This means you are committed to taking action even though it means you will need to be vulnerable. If you still aren't sure, I suggest making a list side by side. What are the benefits of looking at your thoughts, emotions, strengths, and challenges? Then list what would be the negatives. I think you'll see the pros outweigh the cons.

2. Be open minded and meet with a few therapists if you need to. This is your life—don't settle. There is a therapist out there for you. And if this is your first time don't overthink it and put pressure on yourself. Create a list of issues you would like help with. Tell the therapist what you would like to get out of your sessions. This should help you determine if he or she is the right fit. Just relax and be yourself!

3. There's no "right" way to journal because it's very personal, but here's a few basic tips to keep in mind as you're embarking on the world of journaling. Write honestly and openly and just let it flow. This is a

safe place and no is judging you. Don't worry about details like grammar, just write your thoughts and feelings. This will be so impactful to look back on as you progress through your journey. And lastly, write by hand. It makes a difference!

4. Affordability: to those who may not be able to afford therapy, there are a few options that might be of help. First, if you have health insurance see if your provider includes mental health counseling (therapy) and if you can pay a co-pay rather than the therapist's full fee. There also may be community counseling centers in your area who offer sliding scale services (similar to "pay what you can"). If you live by a college or university, you may want to see if they have master's and doctorate level students (on their way to being licensed as a therapist) who are being supervised by a licensed professional. These students need to complete hours in training toward their licensure and under proper supervision might be able offer you low-cost to free counseling (see the university's policy on this by calling the school's counseling office). Some counseling centers or universities offer group therapy for a variety of issues (rage, domestic violence, teen pregnancy, and more) and this could be a free or low-cost option. Lastly, teletherapy is on the rise. Some therapists offer Skype sessions at a lower rate than if you went to see them in person.

Glow Girl Affirmation:
The past is not a reflection of my future.

Are You A Saver?

"The worst thing is to watch someone you love drown and not being able to convince them that they can save themselves by standing up."

—*Anonymous*

BET YOU THOUGHT this chapter was going to be about saving money or hoarding. Nope, that's for another book! This chapter is more serious than finance tips or clutter and one that was challenging for me to write. It's intensely personal and I'm pushing myself to the vulnerability limit on this one. Since that's what I'm asking you to do, I need to do that too.

This is an extremely difficult chapter mostly because it's one of the most important chapters. It's sharing many details of my life that I have previously chosen to keep secret. I kept everyone in the dark on this for so long, I almost lost myself in it. I have worked tremendously hard to grow to where I am today. It's my purpose to share my message, my experience, and what I've learned and nothing in this chapter is meant to be vindictive or hurtful to anyone. I am writing this only out of love and from my heart. If I can help just one woman with my message, then mission accomplished. It's tough to pull back the curtain sometimes out of fear or embarrassment, but we need to own our story and tell it like it is. And if I can be someone's light in their darkness through my story, then it needs to be told.

So, let's begin with a question. Why do we stay in a relationship when we know it's not healthy? Fear of being alone, not wanting to give up, our vows, what our friends will think, feeling like a failure, your children, and not knowing how, might all be valid reasons. Well, sister, mine were all of the above.

I never had a good example of a successful marriage, so I tried to create the picture of what I thought a successful marriage was. In the beginning there were lots of sparks, so it was easier, but the red flags were still there, I just chose to ignore them time and time again. I made the justification that he must really love me because even though he said mean and hurtful things to me, he would beg for forgiveness the next day and was so remorseful. I felt bad. I wanted this to work and I felt I could make it work because I've seen dysfunctional marriages and I could handle whatever came my way.

I knew dysfunction. My parents' divorce when I was seven, then living with an abusive stepfather for five years, and then their divorce at the age of fourteen. When I was about eleven years old, I vividly remember a nice day the three of us had picking apples. Shortly after we got home, my mom and stepfather were arguing in the kitchen and I could hear that it was escalating. Just writing this I can feel my heart beating fast, like it was yesterday. I would normally run and hide, but this day I was feeling particularly courageous and I couldn't listen to it anymore. Enough is enough.

I went out to the garage where we had left the baskets of apples and picked up a basket full of apples. I carried them into the kitchen shaking the entire way and when I turned the corner my stepfather was about to hit my mom and I saw a knife next to him on the counter. I mustered up every bit of courage I had, walked up behind him and yelled, "Get away from my mom now. *Stop*!"

He turned around in shock. I was incredibly shy so for me

to take this bold move was something he would have never imagined I would do. Hell, it was something *I* never imagined I would do! But there I was shaking like a leaf, ready to throw a basket of apples I could barely hang onto at a burly six-foot-tall man to stop him from abusing my mother. I can't say that it stopped him forever, but it stopped him that day. I think it was more because I shocked the hell out of him. A couple of years later when he pushed me down on the kitchen floor, my mom decided we needed to leave. This was what I learned, and this is what I was coming into my marriage with.

This criterion was all I had when I thought about relationships and marriage. I won't let anyone treat me like my stepfather treated my mom. I will marry someone who will respect and cherish me. Someone who will protect me and have my back. Someone who will love me unconditionally. There's so much I want to tell that twenty-year-old me now. But all the challenges brought me to where I am. And without the challenges I don't know that I would be who I am today. I'm thankful for my struggles because without them, I wouldn't have found my strength.

Leaving a toxic relationship is hard but staying in it is even harder.

I realized that *I* was the only one responsible for the type of love I brought into my life. I believe that my husband and I came together because of who were. Flaws and all. I felt so much compassion for my him and I just wanted to be there for him and heal his wounded soul with love in a way no one had been able to love him before.

I thought I could heal him. That I could be his medicine. But then I realized he didn't want to get better.

We can't love people past all their wounds. Because as we are trying to heal their wounds, they are creating wounds in us. Deep devasting wounds. Wounds that will take a long time to heal. Wounds that could ultimately destroy you. Listen to me, sister. Don't let that happen.

What's important to remember is that it's not your love they need. It's their own. You will never be able to "fix" anyone and it's not your job. It's up to us to realize that.

Broken people who refuse to seek help break you.

They can't help it. I lived like that for years thinking I could fix him, until I was almost completely broken. I managed to put some of my pieces together and literally dragged myself to a support group, crying the entire way. It was so scary. This was the first time I met anyone who was going through what I was. It was such an unexplainable feeling. There were other women just like me. Some in worse situations than me. The feeling of camaraderie filled my heart, but at the same time my heart broke for the other women. How was it that I could want the best for them, but not myself?

As Brené Brown says: "Only when we are brave enough to explore the darkness will we discover the infinite power of our light." That's what I refer to when I say "glow." It wasn't until I went deep in the darkness that I discovered I wasn't being true to myself and I wasn't being respected because I didn't think I deserved it. Once I acknowledged these discoveries my flame started to flicker again, and I could feel my glow coming back.

But it was a long and painful process. Without the support of my therapist and patient friends with open hearts, I don't know that I would've ever broken free. I stayed for longer than I know I should have. I wanted it to work and I learned that I was co-dependent. Once I understood that, I began learning and growing, but he was still staying the same.

Again, you can't make someone change or change them. Hurt people, hurt people.

I gave until I had nothing left.

I felt so alone. I isolated myself because I felt I couldn't talk to anyone about what was going on. I thought, what would they think of my husband and then what would they think of me? This was my secret until I discovered a special group for loved ones of people living with addiction. It took a lot of courage to go and open up to a group of people I never even met. But being in a place that was a safe and loving environment allowed me to finally take my guard down. This was an honest atmosphere where our common struggles could be shared with no judgment. Only support.

So, while you may feel as though you are completely alone in your situation—it's important to know that there are many, many other spouses and partners out there who are dealing with similar problems.

The façade was slowly crumbling with each meeting I pushed myself to go to. I could start to feel little pieces of myself coming to the surface and slowly but surely, I could feel the transformation. I could see myself in the other women in the group and I wanted to shake them and say, "You don't deserve this," and the reality was that I wasn't only telling them, but I was also telling myself.

Here was my epiphany and I want you all to read this twice especially if this resonates with you. *I spent so much time trying to figure out why he did the things he did, but I finally realized what I needed to figure out is why I didn't feel like I deserved more than what he was giving me.*

I started reclaiming those elements that I was willing to sacrifice or disregard to make my marriage work. When you surrender so much of your authentic self, you allow subtle erosion of your self-worth and spirit, and gradually "who you really are" almost completely disappears.

It's not a good relationship if you repeatedly feel bad.

If your partner, or potential partner, speaks to you in a way you'd never let someone else speak to you, why do you put up with it? Don't tolerate less than you deserve.

Courage doesn't mean that you don't get afraid. Courage means that you don't let fear stop you.

Walking away shows personal strength and the courage to stand on your own two feet. But at the same time, this was one of the scariest times in my life because if I truly was going to end this marriage, I was ending something I wanted to work so badly. So, did I try hard enough? Was I responsible for destroying my family? What about how I told myself and my husband that I'm only getting married once and it will be forever. Being a child of divorce, I refused to put my child through that. In retrospect now, that was probably the biggest reason I tried everything to make it work.

How could I say (and mean it) that I don't deserve to be treated this way when I didn't even know who I was.

I wrote every day in my journal while I was going through this and as each month passed, I went back to what I wrote, and I could see how I was gaining strength and clarity. Eventually, I knew I had to let go because holding on to a toxic relationship prevents personal growth and I knew wanted to continue to grow. But I also knew I couldn't get to where I knew I *could* go staying in it, unless he was willing to do the same. He wasn't. I knew it was time for me to end this cycle.

Are you in a relationship or marriage with someone who is toxic, narcissistic, or struggling with addiction?

Staying in a relationship like this has so many negative effects if the person is not willing to get help or trying to change. Without learning to love themselves, hurtful people spend their lives trying to get the love they're missing inside from someone else. That someone else is often a sensitive person. Don't let that person be you.

They will take your sympathy, but they don't want to change. They don't want their problems solved, their addictions and distractions taken away, their stories resolved, or their messes cleaned up. Because what would they have left? They don't know and they aren't ready to know yet. And it's not your job to tell them.

Never make yourself feel like nothing to make someone else feel like everything.

I was attending a personal growth conference last year (more about the conference in a later chapter) and I had an unexpected experience. One of my favorite speakers was on stage and she was talking about how now it's time to go after that we really want. She was asking the audience some questions and one woman in particular stood out. She was saying how she did everything she could to get herself to this conference. But her husband was against it and she wasn't even really sure how she was going to continue. You could hear the pain in her voice. The speaker and the audience commended her for getting herself to the conference even despite her challenges.

She was in tears and shared how unhappy she was, but she felt stuck. The speaker questioned her on being "stuck" and began to say things to encourage her to step up and make a change. To believe that she's worth more. That's she's enough just as she is. Through her continued tears, she shared how she can't make a change because she's working in her husband's business and he needed her. She said this was why she shouldn't have come to the conference because she was abandoning him when he needed her there to take care of things.

Many of us were in shock and for me personally her words hit my inner core. I could feel exactly what she was feeling. It's a feeling that you can't imagine any possible way to make a change or even imagine what your life would look like if you did.

She then continued to say that she spoke to her husband that morning to tell him about the conference and that he said to six mean things to her. Just that statement alone broke my heart. Not so much about the mean things, since we all know that happens, but the fact that there were six and even more so, that she knew the exact number. I mean if it's six in only one morning how many is it in a day; twenty, twenty-five, or forty? Did she count them on a regular basis?

She was on the other side of the room filled with hundreds of people and all I wanted to do was run over and hug her and tell her that it's going to be okay. Tell her that there *is* a light at the end of the tunnel. Tell her that it's going to take a lot of work, but she can do it. If I can do it, she can do it too. I became so emotional. I cried for her and most likely for me too.

Her story deeply impacted me. I knew deep down inside at that moment that I want to help women know that they can change their life. I realized I have a gift; a calling and I believe that God has put this on my heart.

As I said earlier, this is such an important message for me to share. I want to let you know, if you are struggling or feeling trapped, I hear you and I feel you. I understand it's so scary and unimaginable how you could create a healthy and fulfilling life away from the toxic place you are right now—there are so many reasons not to make a move. SO many.

What I learned to do because it was so overwhelming to think about it all collectively, was take each reason one by one. When you realize that they're not that huge individually, you start to see that you actually can tackle them or find solutions for whatever that challenge is that's keeping you and holding you there. One by one, step-by-step you start to realize that you can do this.

No one should ever feel imprisoned in a relationship of any kind where their peace of mind, emotional and physical health or safety is compromised. You are a unique and beautiful woman with so much to offer, and you owe it to yourself (and your children, if you have them) to find that special someone who sees and loves you for you, not what they think you should be. You don't need someone to complete you. You only need someone to love and accept you completely.

You are worthy and deserving of love. Love that builds you up and does not make you feel less than. You are worthy of a healthy relationship.

Is this what you dreamed of when you were a child?

I wanted to believe in the fairytale. I wanted to believe in the love story—that we would "make it" and live happily ever after.

I always dreamed of a happily ever after. I'm all about romance. I am a sucker for Hallmark movies! I seriously strive to find my Hallmark romance. Okay, I know they're not real. That's what my son tells me every time he sees me on the couch watching TV with tears in my eyes and a mound of crumpled tissues next to me.

But the truth is, it gives me hope now. Especially when my marriage of eighteen years ended, and I'm left wondering if there are any good guys left out there. It's scary to be single again, in this new online dating world and all those negative thoughts come to your mind, like: *who's going to love me when I'm wrinkly, I'm so old now maybe it's past the point of no return,* and *I should just get a cat and call it a day.* So sad, right?

But I do know, it's better to be alone than to be with someone who's hurting you.

Through the struggles, I know what I deserve now. Your partner should always treat you with respect. That means listening to you, and really paying attention to what you're saying. It means considering your needs and taking them seriously, letting you know how important you are, and being there for you when you need them. Your partner should always, always be honest with you and not keep things from you. If any of those elements are missing, move on. These are red flags. You can do better.

Don't collect red flags. When a man shows you who he is, believe it. After that first red flag, don't stick around for more.

What you allow is what will continue.

Forgive yourself for relationships that you allowed when you didn't know your true worth.

You deserve honesty. You deserve transparency. You deserve someone who respects you enough to not lie to your heart. You deserve appreciation. You deserve loyalty. You deserve someone who would never abuse your trust. You deserve someone who would still be there for you, even if when everyone else has walked away. You deserve joy. You deserve peace.

If anything costs you your peace, then it too expensive.

If it's couple's therapy or if you see a glimmer of hope that the relationship can be fixed, then by all means try to make it work. But please don't hold on and stay in a miserable relationship because you think there will be no one else. You've got to believe you are worth more than being hurt by someone. Believe that someone will see your worth and treat you the way you should be treated. Also, don't fall into the trap of staying because he or she "needs" you. You may find that person needs you more when they think you're slipping away.

You are not responsible for someone else's journey. Only your journey. You don't need someone to tell you how kind and wonderful you are. Give that to yourself. Know your beautiful amazingness and what you have to offer someone. Do the inner-work and build up your strength.

Remember, you are entirely up to you.

There's a difference between giving up and knowing when you have had enough, and you *are* enough. Divorce may be the best option for you to have a better life. We need to stop thinking of it as punishment and start seeing it as a path to a joyous and peaceful life. This path begins with the death of a relationship, which is preceded by a period of sadness and mourning, then followed by a time of rebuilding self-esteem and confidence and ends with the rebirth of an independent strong person.

It's your time now. Who are you, what do you like, what

do you enjoy, what do you want, what do you feel? Rediscover yourself; think about who you were before you stepped into this toxic relationship. Reinvent your life.

Walking away is so difficult, I know that. Ending my marriage was one of the hardest things I ever had to do. Being alone is a scary thought. But being alone and being lonely are not the same thing. Don't be afraid to walk away from someone who leaves your heart heavy, brings you down, and diminishes your flame. Losing someone who doesn't respect or appreciate you is actually a gain, not a loss.

Know the greatness you bring to the table and don't be afraid to eat alone.

A toxic person is great at using your flaws against you, to scare you to stay. They can spot your weaknesses like a hawk. Slowly, one day at a time, I began to stand up for myself. The more you stand up for yourself and rebel, the more you take power way from them.

Letting go feels like giving up. And I am not a quitter; never have been. But walking away from a toxic relationship is quite the opposite. It shows personal strength.

If you are in a toxic relationship, are you being told lies to keep you there? Things like, *you won't make it without me, how are you going to be able to handle the kids by yourself, no one else will want you.* These are lies created to not only keep you but keep you down. Don't listen. Preparation is the key to overcoming and the potential backlash. If you have solutions in place, then the lies will no longer scare you because you have a plan.

I had been seeing my therapist for a couple of years and for months I had been talking about ending my marriage. I knew it was what I needed to do but it was so difficult to get the courage, especially after all the things that were said subtly to keep me in it.

Here is a journal entry from the day I knew I needed to ask my husband to leave:

I went to see Todd (my therapist) today and I'm honestly so sick and tired of talking about this (separating). I know I need to confront him once and for all. Todd asked me what I was afraid of and I really had to think about it. I just want it to go smoothly. I'm afraid of what he's going to say. I'm worried about him making me feel bad. Then Todd put it into perspective. Why am I afraid he's going to be angry with me or think I'm a bad person? Who is he to judge me? Boom!

I realized that I would always second guess myself and now I needed to trust myself.

Confronting a narcissist is like going into battle. Therefore, you need to be prepared to go into battle. Stay strong and don't take anything that's said to you personally. Remember, this is coming from a wounded person.

As some of you may know, this process is not an easy one. There are so many emotions involved and for me even though I ended it, the death of the relationship period took so much longer, because for that first year I was hoping he would have an epiphany and realize everything he was losing, get help, and fight like hell to save the marriage and his family. That never happened and I struggled with the *why*. Big time.

As I was hoping that he would realize what he lost and beg for me to try to make it work, then I had an epiphany. Is he the kind of man right now I'm hoping will fight for me?

The reality is the core of who your partner was before he met you is who he is. I clung onto the idea that he would change once he could truly feel my love, my loyalty, and my patience. However, you can't change the fundamentals of who someone is; that is a choice they have to make for themselves.

The longer we chase the "wrong" person, the less time we have for the "right" person.

Let go of trying to figure out why they do what they do.

And sister, I still struggle with that at times, but please don't let it take you over. Find the courage to let go of what you cannot change and the courage to change the things you can. Know they will never operate by logic and once you accept it, you will begin to break through.

The best thing I did was learn to stop fighting for someone who was okay with losing me.

If you have been in a destructive relationship, then you have wounds that have to heal. Healing takes time. Don't blame yourself! You are probably angry, mixed with a lot of other feelings like betrayal. You may have turned into a different person than you were before. And you don't like the person you are now. It is important to accept these feelings for your healing process. You need this to recover yourself again.

The healing road is long but know you are built for this journey.

Sometimes you have to let go of the picture of what you thought life would be like and learn to find joy in the new story you're living.

Now is the time to regain control over your life and learn to trust yourself again. You have to regain your strength and set new boundaries.

You don't find your worth in a romantic partner; you find your worth within yourself and then you find a romantic partner who is worthy of you.

I know now, I will never let anyone treat me or talk to me in a degrading manner. I will not accept to be treated less than. I refuse to be manipulated.

I now look at my present situation with gratitude. It was opportunity to learn and discover things about myself. I know that I am not a failure. Divorce is the failure of a marriage to survive.

When my marriage ended, I struggled to see the positives

at times even with all the work I was doing. I was so exhausted from trying to fix my marriage, the struggle to encourage him to see what was happening and trying to keep the peace. I lost important parts of myself along the way; I needed time to reclaim those parts and acknowledge the new me and my new life.

I wanted my marriage to work more than anything. I worked so hard to save it. I loved my husband and was heartbroken we couldn't make this work. I was grateful for all the good times and fun memories. I was grateful for the gift of giving me my beautiful son.

But it is my decision that I will allow my divorce to transform me into someone bolder and stronger.

It was time to move on. I had a second chance to rebuild my life and while I was heartbroken it wasn't the life I had previously dreamed of and imagined; it was now a wide-open road of possibilities which is so exciting but can be scary at the same time. So much unknown. I am so grateful and blessed for the support of my friends and family, even my in-laws who are my family too.

Some people in my life who never took the time to know the story were so quick to judge me. Since my beverage business was growing, the assumption was that I didn't need my husband anymore or that he can't give me what I need now since I must have such high expectations. My expectations have always been the same and are simple. To respect me and treat me kindly. To protect me and love me with all your heart. I know now that they are not my true friends. My true friends are right by my side.

Don't let judgment from others stop you from progressing forward to your greatness. Your worth does not revolve around other people's opinions of you. People will judge us for the choices we make without even knowing the options we had to choose from.

It's been three years now and I feel gratitude and appreciate what I learned from my marriage. I learned I am more capable than I thought. I did a lot without my husband and doing things solo can be harder at times, but it's also empowering. I've accomplished a lot, encountered many challenges, but I worked hard and I'm here. I survived and I'm so proud of my accomplishments.

While I thought my happily ever after was going to be spent with my husband going on adventures together and experiencing life as a team, going to all the places we talked about once our son started college; it's become a different kind of "adventure" now. My mess is now my message. My struggles are now my voice. My purpose is now my adventure.

I create healthy boundaries now, I've stepped way outside my comfort zone, and I've shown my son what it means to stand up for yourself and how to be resilient in the face of adversity. Through the work I've done, I understand my part in our co-dependent relationship and I'm more confident and independent now. I know what I want now, and I know what I deserve. I have a voice.

My purpose is to help as many women as I can through my story. It took me a long time to finally share it, but by opening up and being honest about my experiences and healing, I've realized that not only have I helped myself move on, but I'm also helping others see light in the darkness.

Release yourself from any toxic relationships and step back into the light. Experience life outside of the darkness. Learn to love yourself again and live your best life. You're worth it.

There's nothing more empowering than learning to love yourself.

Focus on your positive qualities. Recognize your accomplishments. Even small ones. Give yourself credit for standing up for yourself. For believing in yourself.

Write in a journal to get your feelings out and develop

an awareness of who you are, your feelings and your beliefs. Read back over what you've written every few weeks so you can see how you're reacting to certain situations. Create some positive affirmations like, *I am not responsible for the end of my marriage. I am a fully capable parent and I love my children. I see my situation now as an opportunity for growth. I have so much to offer because I've taken the time to learn. I know what I deserve now and won't accept anything less.*

Look for people who are close to you and who will understand. People who can support you and who you trust. My close friends were there for me each step of the way. They listened to me, supported me, and comforted me through many tears. Don't be afraid to lean on a friend or family member.

Taking care of yourself and loving yourself will give you strength you may have never known existed within you.

Your real self has been waiting for you. Your life is your creation and sometimes the scariest most courageous life changing things are not about doing them, but to stop doing them.

I'm here to tell you sister, ending a toxic relationship is never easy but if you put in the work you will begin to see the light shining though the storm clouds that darkened your life.

Soon the dark clouds begin to fade in to the beautiful bright blue sky you've been hoping to see for so long and you will shine again.

There is only one person in this world that you can change—and that's you.

A few of my favorite tips to help you move on and heal from toxic relationships...

1. Make sure you realize that you are the most important person in your life and make time for *yourself*. Book a trip with a friend. Pick a place you've always wanted to

go and do it! If you have children, plan a special trip with them. Explore new places, go to a concert, dance, shop, swear, sing, make a new friend, paint, pursue your passion. Go do the things you love! Dream a new dream. It's important you enjoy life again.

2. Find a nurturing support group or therapist. Share your story. It's so important to not feel isolated and once we begin sharing it opens the doors to freedom. I encourage you to seek out a support group where you can share your feelings in a safe environment. Don't be afraid to ask for help, just take that first step. There are resources and people out there who can help and who want to help. You don't have to go through it alone! Empower yourself; read books, journal, listen to podcasts.

3. Write a goodbye letter. I did this and it really helped. I said goodbye to all the memories that I thought we would still be making and all our inside jokes, special places, dreams we had like going to Tuscany, our holiday traditions I loved so dearly, our family time, and special things only he and I shared. Getting all of them out released them. Instead of the memories popping up every so often, I acknowledged them. I thanked them for being a part of my life and I'm ready to move on now and create new memories with my son. You can choose to save the letter, give it to your spouse, or release it by discarding it. Whatever works best for you.

Glow Girl Affirmation:
I let go of all that no longer serves me.

9

LOSS

"Grief is in two parts. The first is loss. The second is the remaking of life."

—*Anne Roiphe*

Loss. How CAN you *gain* through loss? I was determined to answer this question.

The day my dad was unexpectedly diagnosed with brain cancer was one of the worst days of my life. I would be forever changed.

A girl's first true love is her father. It's been a few years since my dad's passing, but I remember it like it was yesterday. One minute he was so healthy and active, walking five miles on the beach every day, then suddenly he was diagnosed with a life-threatening disease. One year later he was gone.

My dad was extremely fit, and he loved the outdoors. You would find him outside any given day walking or riding his bike. And it didn't matter if it was hot or cold, he would be outside in shorts. That was his "signature" look, even if it was snowing. He loved the beach, walking, and Dunkin' Donuts coffee; in no particular order. And he loved the clothing brand Life is Good. A pair of shorts, a Life is Good T-shirt, and a coffee in hand, "life was good" for him. Until it wasn't.

He fought with tremendous grit, dignity, and bravery but finally the cancer took over. It was a battle and I wanted to help him fight it. Being an only child, I tried incredibly hard to balance being there for him, my son, my friends, and still grow my business. It was a whirlwind. Somehow, I managed but sometimes I was not successful at it. It was one of the most difficult times in my life. He was angry cancer was happening to him and there wasn't anything I could do to fix it or make it better.

He was my dad and he was leaving me. My dad who is smart, witty, stoic, prideful, patent creator, hard-working. The dad who saw me every weekend when I was little, who took me on road trips and said I was the best map reader, who would wait at McDonald's for me to get a plain cheeseburger, who took me to where the Olympics were held, who played every board game I ever wanted, who went sledding with me and at the bottom of every trip said, "Get on and I'll pull you back up." He was an amazing Pop-Pop to my son. They were two peas in a pod. I still remember working in my home office and hearing gut busting laughter coming from the two of them for hours outside my office door.

I wondered how I could handle his death. I nearly had a breakdown when he decided to have brain surgery. My dad was in the hospital for a week and the day he was scheduled for surgery they took him in early. I promised him I would be there before he went in. They called me as I was nearing the hospital and said they were sorry, but they couldn't wait...they were bringing him in. I sped up to the front of the hospital and jumped out of my car and ran, not caring where I parked. I finally got to the right floor and they said they already took him back to surgery and no one was allowed in.

That's when my breakdown happened. Full on hyperventilating. Hysterical. A nurse happened to be walking by me and looked concerned, as anyone would be after seeing someone in my condition. He asked me if I needed help and I explained the situation in between my tears and shortness of breath.

He whispered, "Wait here." He made a phone call to someone in surgery (who just happened to be a good friend of his, I found out later). In my hysterics, it was hard to make out what they were discussing, but he hung up and softly said, "Follow me."

He took my hand and we went through a door. He and another guy dressed me in scrubs in a closet while I tried to calm down. I had no idea what was happening. They said nothing and I just let them dress me. The mask was the final piece to my "costume." They opened the door and the nurse whispered into my ear for me to walk with them and walk fast with my head down.

The next thing I knew we came up to double doors and we went in. There was my dad. He was lying flat on his back on a stretcher in the center of a big cold room filled with all types of equipment and many people were scurrying around him. His surgeon and others all looked stunned. They were just giving him anesthesia and he turned his head towards the door. I saw intense fear in his face. I had never seen him look like this. I will never forget it. I quickly pulled my mask down and said, "Dad it's me!" I could see big tears beginning to roll softly down his cheek.

"I made it," I said. "I told you I would be here." It took every ounce of strength I had to try not to cry. I wanted to be strong for him. I knew he was about to go under anesthesia and have a large tumor removed from his brain. I wanted him to know he was going to get through this. I walked over to him and he slowly extended his arm towards me. I took his hand in mine and he squeezed hard. Looking in his tear-filled eyes I saw something. Something that said, thank you for being here and for being my daughter.

Just then, I was abruptly told I needed to leave right away. The nurse walked me out and helped me get out of the scrubs. I found out he could have lost his job because of what he did.

I hugged him. He was my angel. I met many angels on the journey with my dad and gave me an incredible gift that I will be forever grateful for.

Life is full of surprises, good and bad. You never know what future holds. What news you'll get, how things might drastically change in a matter of a week, month, or year. You'll never know who you will cross your path, who will be there unexpectedly in a desperate time of need, what things you will experience, or how many new stories you will create.

My dad thankfully came out of surgery and recovered extremely well but more tumors grew only a month later. It was a scary time for him and for me. He was angry that he could not fix this, and I was trying to be there for him in the best way that I knew how. I was an only child living three states away and in the heart of growing a business, raising a son, in the middle of a troubled marriage no one knew about, including my dad. And he had no one else close by.

He lived with me while he recovered and once he was feeling better he wanted to go back home. He definitely didn't like me hovering over him and we had aides coming in every day to help with rehab after brain surgery.

Shortly after he went back home, he started to get worse again and we learned the smaller tumors were now bigger. He was in the same spot he was two months prior before having a large tumor removed. It was so disappointing after going through all that to discover he had more tumors. They wouldn't operate again so we tried to just keep him comfortable but the more the cancer progressed the angrier he became, and it was easiest to take it out on me because I was closest to him. And I couldn't be there with him all the time like he wanted because of everything else going on in my life.

We hired in-home care and that wasn't going well. I told him I would try to fix it, but we couldn't seem to find him the right caregiver. Thankfully, a manager at the home care service,

Donna, saw what was happening and she stepped in to help on her own time. I don't even have words for all that she did for my dad. She was so selfless and went above and beyond to help. She made sure whenever she could that my dad had what he needed. We talked often and we became incredibly close. Donna is a true angel.

My dad grew more and more angry with me and I tried to do anything I could to ease the pain for him, but it wasn't working. It broke my heart, but I prayed and prayed for serenity for him. I knew at that time he didn't have much longer.

Soon, I received a call when I was at a tradeshow in Chicago from Donna and she said she had to tell me what happened earlier that day. I thought it was going to be something bad as usual, so I braced myself. She proceeded to tell me that my dad asked to go to Whole Foods (his favorite store) that day and so she took him. The back story to this is that my dad never really liked that I started my beverage brand because it was so much work and he worried about me and my stress, along with all the travel and pressure. I tried to explain to him that this was my dream. To grow a big brand and see it on store shelves all through the U.S. When I told him this, he would always ask me, "Well…is it in Whole Foods?" I would answer, "Not yet dad," feeling defeated and like he would not recognize it as *anything* until it got in Whole Foods. Needless to say, I worked hard to get it in there and I did it. We got in Whole Foods *and* it was in the store he shopped. By the time it happened he was in his final months and I didn't even know if he completely comprehended it was there.

Donna told me that while she and Dad were in the soda aisle at Whole Foods he specifically sought out and found Sipp and asked that she pick up a four pack. She was surprised at his request since she knew he never even tried it before—in the five years since I started the company. I was in tears. *Was this really happening*, I thought? Then when they went to checkout, she said he was telling the cashier about how this was his daughter's beverage. About how I created it and pointed out my signature on the bottle. My mind was blown, and I was a sobbing mess. And when they got home Dad, her, and the nurse's aide all drank the four pack and he loved it.

I collapsed on my bed in my hotel room sobbing. Things had been so strained between me and my dad. This was a gift from God. I flew out the next morning and called him as soon as I got home to tell him I was driving up to Connecticut to see him the next day. As soon as I heard his voice, I wanted to talk about the Whole Foods trip. He did too. He said how happy he was to see it and how much he loved it. I cried and thanked him. I told him how much it meant to me that he wanted to try it. I could feel the anger I typically heard from him slowly dissipate as we were talking. We were having a deep connection. He then said, "Honey...I'm so proud of you," with his crackly voice and I could feel his emotion and pride through the phone. He had just given me the biggest gift of all.

In that moment I felt that he was not only proud of what I accomplished, but he was also proud of *me*. It's a moment I will never forget.

That following week we made arrangements for him to come to Pennsylvania because we knew we were in the final months. I spoke to him the night before we left. On our drive up we received a phone call that he fell while he was getting ready and couldn't get up, so they had to call the ambulance. When we got to the hospital I rushed in and he was in the ER in lots of pain. They felt something happened when he fell, and he was not in any condition to make the trip to Pennsylvania. I broke down and cried like I have never cried.

I tried to talk to him, but he was incoherent, and I wasn't sure if he heard me. The hospital recommended that we have him transferred to hospice. At that point I knew it was the end and he wasn't going to come home with me. I think I was in a temporary state of shock. I made the decision to stay with him in Connecticut as long as I needed to and to be by his side. He was in hospice for a week and being there with him was one of the hardest and most horrific things I've ever been through.

After he fell that morning, he never spoke again. Cancer took him from me. I sat with him talking on and off, just hoping he could hear me, trying to make sure he was comfortable and playing his favorite jazz music every day.

I never imagined how much strength it would take to stay by his side watching him suffer as I was trying everything I could possibly do to *stop* the suffering.

I know the only way I made it through the most heart wrenching week of my life was Donna. While we were with my dad in those final days, we would tell him that we were both there together. She was by my side every day at hospice. She brought me food, comforted me, shared stories with me about my dad that I didn't even know, told me all the nice things he would say about me to her, held me when I cried, and gave me a break when I needed to leave the room because I couldn't listen to him being in pain.

Donna was my rock and I couldn't have done it without her. I will be forever grateful. When the nurses saw us together, they thought she was my sister—and she is.

While it was a journey of anger, emotions, tears, fear, and sadness...my dad and I connected like we never had before in the end. He gave me many gifts throughout my life but in the end the gift that was most special and the one I'll never forget was when he told me, "I'm so proud of you." I hear it now over and over and it continues to give me the strength to persevere and fly!

I miss my dad every day, but if I only focused on the loss of my dad, then I would not see the gifts that came from it.

Life itself is a gift. We all have so much to be grateful for, no matter what has happened in our lives. I am grateful for our memories and for "the gift" he gave me towards the end.

And I am grateful for what I've learned through his loss. It has brought me here today and given me a new purpose to impact women's lives, and to create a community of women who would like to rise up to greatness in their lives.

If you are reading this right now from a place of grief, I feel for you. You're going to get through this. Grieving is a process, and everyone goes through it differently. Grief comes in waves. Some are rough and some are calm. Sometimes you know it's coming and sometimes you don't. Some days the wave of grief can wash over you like a mean tidal wave knocking you off your feet. Especially when certain memories pop in your head. Just try to ride the wave until it's over. Remember, this is *your* process to deal with in whatever way you can—so don't feel compelled or pressured to act a certain way because you feel that's what's expected. There is no "proper" timeframe for grief either. It takes however long it takes even if some people in your life say otherwise.

For me, I knew that if I didn't focus on the "gift" my dad gave me, our angel Donna, and the support of family and friends, it would have been even more painful. If you're currently struggling through a loss, I encourage you to reach out to someone for support. And just remember, even though your loved one may no longer be with us here on earth, they live on in our hearts. I hope you can find even a small comfort in that.

The loss of my dad was a wakeup call and I decided that living my life to the fullest was and is the greatest way I can honor him. Also, life is too short to not stand up for myself, not to love people more, to appreciate what I have, to not be afraid. Because seeing the fear in my dad's eyes knowing he was going to die, put it all into perspective. If I'm afraid to put myself out there and do what I truly want, what's the worst that could happen? Someone might not like it? Perspective is one of the greatest gifts we can give ourselves.

I held onto one of my dad's favorite Life is Good T-shirts and it's a constant reminder that the "good" life begins right now when you stop waiting for a better one.

Take it and don't wait and see if it comes to you or think you can't do it. We have so many possibilities and opportunities in front of us. My dad wanted to retire to Florida, and he looked at places for years, but he just couldn't decide. Would he have let all that time pass if he knew what his future would hold? Year after year floated by and when he was finally getting close to deciding, it was when he was diagnosed with cancer.

Would you be happy with your life if you knew you only had one more day to live? My dad's passing jolted me to reflect and think about my future.

The possibilities are endless as to what could happen, but many of us don't think about it until something actually does happen. We live our lives like we can predict when we'll die. But we can't. We tend to allow life to simply happen to us. Why are we standing by and allowing our most valuable resource to deplete every day and not fighting to live the life we truly want to live?

Why do we keep our dream life as only a dream? Why don't we do something about it?

No more dreams. Make your dreams a reality. Live like you want. Say things to loved one you've always wanted to say. Now is your time. We never know when things will change. When great opportunities could just pass us by, and we won't have a second chance. When something we take for granted could be taken away.

We don't know when later will be too late.

Just before I started writing this book, I was told I had to have a biopsy on a cyst that could possibly be cancerous. Not the words anyone wants to hear. Thankfully it came back clear but waiting for the results was brutal. It definitely forces you to look at what's most important, which is why I can't emphasize enough that life is short and fragile.

Don't do things that make you unhappy. Let go of things that aren't helping you or are hurting you. If you are not happy with something make a change. Please don't waste any more time being unhappy. Trust me sister, I did that and now I can never get those years back. Figure out a solution. Reach out for help if you need to (...and don't be afraid to). You owe it to yourself.

So now I encourage you to take some time to reflect on this. If tomorrow were your last day, what would you do *right* now? Every second would be precious, so you would be pretty selective of how you spend it, right?

You'd realize how much time you'd spent on unimportant things that made you feel good in the moment but would never help to create anything for your future.

Every day you've been given a chance to experience all that life has to offer and by creating the mindset that every day is a gift; you will pay attention to the things that are most important to you. You won't wait until "tomorrow" to do the things you've been wanting to do and you'll "go for it."

What would you say to the people you care about? What is that thing that you've been wanting to start?

Be present. Occupy your life with only the things that matter. Show up to your life and live it. Stand up for yourself, fight for what you believe in, create a mission, invent a product, start a business. Love more, fear less. Let go of grudges. Do that thing that's been lingering in the back of your mind.

Find moments to shine and embrace the people who are a light in your life and make you feel alive. Let them know that they light up your life.

People we love will die. A spouse may leave us. A friend may abandon us. We could lose our business or job. Loss will happen in this world that we can't explain or understand. It's not fair. The one thing we know is that it will be there. Life can't be perfect.

But sister, think of this. If life is about loss, it is also about discovery.

You can transform loss into a gift that allows you to rise above, to be more than what you ever thought you were capable of. Loss is painful, but it reveals what is most important. Within the struggle are the seeds of transformation.

I'm certain there are so many things in your life right now that are worth living for. You have people in your life *right now* that you're taking for granted. You have an endless well of untapped potential within you, just sitting there waiting to be released. There is no next opportunity, only the one right in front of you. Do the things you love, be with the people you love, follow your passion, and pursue your dreams relentlessly.

So, when are you going to start truly living?

Is it going to be "one day" or "day one?" Nothing can stop you once you decide what you want.

Rise up to your greatness because *your* world is waiting for you.

A few of my favorite tips to live like there is no tomorrow...

1. All we truly have is the present, so engage. Take the steps toward creating the life you want right now. You are what you make yourself. Start that novel, paint that masterpiece, start that project, find that new job. Whatever it is, now is the time. Today is the day.

2. Say what you need to say but haven't said. Ask yourself, "What will I regret never saying, to those I love, and to myself?" One of the biggest regrets when someone passes are the words that could have been said but weren't. Don't wait until it's too late. Be vulnerable and

share what's in your heart. Don't wait to tell your loved ones how much you love and support them or how proud you are and that you will always be there for them. Those words are your gift.

3. Forgive. Choose compassion, forgiveness, and reconciliation. If you're holding onto resentment and anger you need to let them go. Life's too short to hold onto grudges. Forgive, and avoid a life of bitterness and anger. You might even miss out on amazing love because sometimes an, "I forgive you," can mend a broken relationship to become even stronger than it was.

Glow Girl Affirmation:
My life is a gift and I appreciate
everything I have.

10

Swipe Right And Go

"Life is either a daring adventure or nothing at all."

—*Helen Keller*

So, SOME OF you may know what swipe right is and some may not. Can I hear all the single ladies out there? I never imagined I would find myself single after eighteen years of marriage, but there I was. Beth: party of one. I had no clue how the new dating world worked. Swiping left or right, hooking-up, LTR (like…left to right, letter size, or long-term relationship—WTF?) …what was all this?

To be honest, I wasn't sure about including this chapter because of the story I'm about to tell. It's a tad bit…how do I say it…*crazy*! But I did say I would be authentic, and this story was life changing so…here it goes. #facepalm Oh, and thank God my mom already knows (you can swipe left on this chapter, Mom)!

So, have you heard of the "Irish exit?" When someone leaves abruptly without saying goodbye. I think I coined a new phrase, called the "Irish entrance." It's as ridiculous as it sounds. It's when someone (me) meets a guy online, talks to him over the phone right before he has a trip to Ireland planned and instead of waiting for him to come back, that person decides to spontaneously enter Ireland to meet him. Hence, the "Irish entrance."

What was that? Did I just hear a gasp of surprise? I hear you. But hey, *he* asked! And with my newly found "just say yes" mentality, how could I possibly say no? I know…the logical thing to do would be wait until he gets back since we only lived twenty minutes apart, but the *much* more exciting choice would be to jump on a plane in a few days and meet in Ireland. So that's what I did. I booked my flight and off I went. Put down the gavel Judge Judy!

This probably was one of the most spontaneous (insane) things I've ever done and if you knew me years ago, I would've *never* made such a bold decision. Never.

Was this a true love connection set in the backdrop of romantic Ireland just like the movie *Leap Year*? Or was he a serial killer? Read on, ladies…

I was beyond excited to arrive in Dublin to meet "him." We'll call him "Mr. Cupid" for the purposes of our story. I arrived at the hotel and met up with a friend who was living in Dublin until Mr. Cupid arrived back from a tour. The anticipation was building. We planned to meet in the hotel bar that night and if you only knew the romantic ideas flowing through my mind at the time. Imagine *this* love story! *This* will put Hallmark to shame, I thought.

Within the first few minutes in the bar, all my romantic ideas stopped flowing through my mind and flew right out of my mind! I mean they flew so far and were never to be seen by anyone in Ireland. Ever.

Let me break it down for you. Was he handsome like in his photos? Check. Did he smile when he greeted me? Check. Did he let me order my drink first? Check. So far so good, right? When he ordered his vodka drink and our waitress didn't know what the brand vodka he asked for, did he politely repeat it or just choose another vodka? No. He became extremely irritated with the waitress, repeated it three times, and when I suggested another brand after she still didn't understand, he emphatically informed me he only drinks *one* brand. I played a game in my mind. How many red flags can I count in the first thirty minutes? Answer: Too many.

It so was disappointing, but I knew I would have to figure out a way to make the best of it. It might not have been the love-at-first sight magic I dreamed of, but still he was a decent guy. I made the decision to keep the tours we had planned for the next few days but tell him how I felt in the morning.

We had to meet at 6 a.m. to take a train and bus to the Cliffs of Moher. The night before I debated on even going since I didn't feel the connection I had hoped, but I flew all the way to Ireland and the Cliffs was one of the main highlights of the trip. I decided to go and knew I had to talk to him on the way. I don't like confrontation and I didn't know him well enough to know how he might react. And what if he was revengeful? I mean, we were on our way to cliffs that stood 700 feet above the Atlantic Ocean for God's sake. But he had to know how I felt so we talked and decided to make the best of it together.

The Cliffs of Moher was the top excursion of his trip and something he had thought out and planned extensively. Numerous times he told me he wanted to go out at least four miles (the Cliffs are massive at about 8.5 miles or 14 kilometers) and it probably wasn't going to be easy but reiterated this was extremely important to him. I think he feared I might hold him back since he was emphasizing how the trek could be extremely precarious, especially in the rain.

He was making such a point about the "treacherous" path, I decided to discreetly research what this was all about on my phone on the bus ride there, Googling, "How many people have fallen of the Cliffs of Moher and died," and proceeded to click the "I'm Feeling Lucky" button in the search bar. The results were not so "lucky." To my surprise several people die each year falling off the cliffs. In fact, to warn visitors of the danger, a memorial statue was placed at the path's trailhead. I was horrified. I thought, *what did I agree to?* And let's be honest here, the most dangerous path I'm most comfortable venturing out on is the paved dog path near my house (if I don't look down, I may step in a dried dog doodie—yikes!).

Even so, I let him know I'm a big girl and if it got too strenuous, I could turn around and head back to wait for him at the visitor center. No biggie! I was already feeling nervous so getting him worked up about my apprehension I knew would not help anyone.

That day it was chilly, misting, windy, and muddy. All the best conditions to walk out on an enormous cliff. When on the bus we missed our stop and ended up getting off at the next stop in a quaint, picturesque village. And there, in all its Irish glory stood the cutest authentic pub only a minute's walking distance from the bus stop. It might have even been glowing. We decided to walk there to see if they knew when the next bus would be coming to go to the Cliffs. When we walked in, I thought I stepped in a pub straight out of a movie. I wandered around admiring all the details and became enveloped by the coziness of it all. The roaring, crackling fire was being stoked by an Irishman who looked like he had been a part of this place his entire life. It was magical to me! I kept telling Mr. Cupid to look at all history, the photos on the wall, and the cozy fire. But each response I got was grumpier than the last, "We need to leave right away!" "Come on!" "The bus is coming in five minutes." My smile turned into a frown. I wasn't ready to leave.

"But look at this fire. Can't we…" I was cut off before I could finish my sentence.

"Let's go," he snapped and briskly walked towards the door to exit.

As we were walking up the hill to the bus stop, I said in my sternest voice that after we walk the cliffs, I would like to take the bus back there to have a beer and something to eat in the pub.

"Why?" was all he could say with the most baffled look on his face.

Mr. Cupid was quickly turning into the Grinch who Stole My Ireland Trip. I needed to choose my next words wisely. But instead, I blurted out, "Because I want to!" He rolled his eyes at me and looked away. That obviously didn't work, so then I took it down a notch and calmly explained, "I've never been in an *authentic* Irish pub and the fireplace was so cozy and it will definitely be nice after being in the cold rain to warm up." Good sales pitch, right?

He reluctantly agreed after rolling his eyes again nearly whining at this point, "Whatever; who travels *all* the way to Ireland to see a *fireplace*...yeesh."

Um...*ME*, that's who (I may have only muttered that under my breath in the moment).

We arrived at the Cliffs and it was still lightly raining and windy, but the weather was a bit better than when we first got to the village. *See, my pub stop helped*, I thought.

We got the lay of the land and he knew where to go and the best side we should walk out on. He told me many times to "dress appropriately" and to bring ear muffs because of the cold wind. The pair of us was truly a sight to behold. Me in my Michael Kors down puffy jacket with gold trim, my purple fuzzy ear muffs, and my lavender striped cashmere scarf. Him in a full zip up hazmat-like body suit with ear muffs, a hat, gloves, and a hood that I think hermitically sealed around his face so absolutely *nothing* could get in—not even empathy and human kindness. Ugh. Oh, and I had gloves with the special finger tips so I could still use my phone and keep them on. When I excitedly showed him to let him know I could use my phone to take pics on the cliffs, he shook his head and said, "Of course, you *would* have *those* gloves."

We made our way to the start of the cliffs and there were two paths. To the right there was a sign that warned visitors to, "Enter at Your Own Risk," with big large red letters at the bottom that spelled, "DANGER." To the left was the side most (sane) people walk which has a protective barrier running along the edge. We decided to venture on the outside of the barrier for most of our trek and I was surprised that *I* agreed to that. It was pretty precarious at times and when we would stop along the way and look back the views were more spectacular with each bend—like nothing I've ever seen in my life. It made me want to keep going even though it was challenging with high winds and extremely slippery in many spots. We continued walking on the barrier-free edge and we both slipped, falling close to the edge multiple times, but we supported each other along the way.

Eventually, I realized that we walked out further than anyone. I totally surprised myself. He asked if I was ready to go back because he felt we went far enough, but I said I wanted to go further. I wanted to take the next bend in the cliff to see what was on the other side. The look on his face was priceless. He was shocked. Hell, I was shocked! *Who is this person I've become on the Cliffs of Moher?* I thought. *What's happening to me in Ireland?* He agreed and we ventured on.

I went curve by curve and I use this analogy in life now: just make it to the next "curve." You never know what spectacular thing you might find or experience. If you truly want to discover the hidden treasures within you and around you, push yourself to the limit.

We passed the next curve and what we saw when we looked back took my breath away. I was in complete awe of the magnificent beauty. I pushed myself beyond the limit and the reward was priceless. We both stood there next to each other gazing out at the view. Speechless. I was overcome by emotion and tears started streaming uncontrollably down my cheeks. It was so unexpected. One week ago, I would have never imagined

I would be in Ireland, never mind standing on the Cliffs of Moher after walking on the dangerous edge with no protective barrier for over four miles. I took a leap of faith and here I was experiencing this stunning moment.

I took a deep breath. Then I thought of my dad. I talked to him in my head and said I wished he was there to see it and I hoped he was seeing it through my eyes. I took in the entire magnificent vision; all for him to see. I wept for him that he didn't have the opportunity to experience all the things he wanted to do and see. I told him I would do it for both us now. The tears were really streaming down my cheeks now. He noticed I was crying and there was a moment of silence and it was quite the moment. Then he interjected with, "Come on! You're not going get all girly on me now, are you?" Um, seriously? How romantic.

We walked back helping each other along the way while taking short breaks to snap some photos. When we got back to the visitor center, I was cold, covered in mud, and completely drenched. But I was incredibly proud of myself. I felt like I could do *anything*—something I had never felt before. My head was spinning, and I was so grateful I had this unbelievable opportunity and I know I wouldn't have gone that far without Mr. Cupid by my side.

The Irish proverb; *May the road rise up to meet you. May the wind always be at your back*, had a whole new meaning for me.

I stepped outside my comfort zone walking on the edge of the cliffs without the barrier and I went further than I ever imagined. I was living life on the edge, literally. It is truly an extraordinary feeling when you challenge yourself do something that might scare you and when you take that chance you discover what's waiting on the other side. Just like if we want to reach our dreams and goals, we need to push through our limits.

I know it's scary to climb that high and let go. But what

if you never do? What if you never see that beautiful, breathtaking view? What if you never get to see what life is like from up there? Don't let "limits" stop you from doing anything.

The comfort zone is a beautiful place, but nothing ever "grows" there.

So…what happened with Mr. Cupid after we walked back? I wouldn't want to leave you with a cliffhanger (pun intended!). I could clearly see by that point that this was no love connection, but I *wanted* to go to that quaint picturesque pub. And I felt like I deserved it after pushing through my comfort zone. I just walked four miles on the edge of a cliff in wind and rain and I wanted to sit in front of a damn friggin authentic Irish pub crackling toasty fireplace! And we did.

The exciting adventure didn't end there for me either. Remember the friend I met up with who was living in Ireland? Well after I told him the infamous quaint pub fireplace story, he surprised me on my last night in Ireland with a personal fireplace tour he created all around Dublin! I was in fireplace heaven. If Mr. Cupid only knew, I think I would have gotten a double eye roll (I wonder if his frequent eye rolls make him dizzy).

My "swipe of faith" and one little word, *yes*, lead me on an incredible and life-changing adventure. So, while this story is about a decision I made after swiping, it's about taking that leap of faith. Think about it. One year = 365 opportunities. Why do we wait or hesitate when every day is an opportunity for a new adventure? Don't let year after year pass you by because you're too busy, you're too afraid or you think it's too late for you. It's never too late.

Have you recently been asked on go on an adventure, but you declined?

Is there a place you want to go or something you want to do, but haven't even started to figure out the details of how to make it happen?

What I found by taking chances is that I broke through something I never thought I could. The key word here is *thought*. Once this happens, suddenly the tapestry of stories you've told yourself about your capabilities starts to unravel, thread by thread.

Then you begin to question, *what other 'thoughts' are not true?* Then your mindset begins to change. And instead of turning down challenging opportunities, you begin to look forward to them. You'll *want* to do them just to see if you can.

It's so exciting to find out what you're truly made of. You begin to see how far you can push your limits. And if you keep going—you'll change. You'll be stronger. You begin to weave a new tapestry of stories. Stories filled with adventure and magical moments. Because once you do that thing you thought was impossible—it no longer is and becomes I'm Possible. That "thing" no longer has any power over you. You're in charge.

Think of the world as a book. How may pages have you read? Start turning the pages and explore and discover. Take every chance you get because some things only happen once. So, take that trip to Paris (hell—start with Paris, Texas if you must) or go on that road trip. The best memories are created when we say, "yes."

The luck of the Irish was on my side by making this bold and daring decision. I left Ireland with the most delightful gift and discovered many things about myself. Taking chances, believing in myself, breaking barriers, being honest, standing up for myself, experiencing beautiful breathtaking moments, and pushing myself beyond my limit.

I felt a sense of freedom. We can be trapped in set of beliefs we created for ourselves that have been formed over the course of many years. I could have easily said I shouldn't go. It might not have been safe. And I had never been to Ireland. But when we learn to let go of how we think things "should" be, let our guard down, think about the possibilities, then we can experience a true sense of freedom and joy.

Don't be a victim of the rules you live by. Leap into the unknown. The hardest part is deciding to leap, the rest is an exhilarating ride with spectacular scenery along the way.

I want you to commit to being the greatest version of *you* and truly live your life fearlessly. Leap into the unknown. It will be the best decision you will ever make.

I promise.

A few of my favorite tips to encourage you to take a leap of faith...

1. Practice small acts of bravery. Taking small steps to break out of your comfort zone slowly builds confidence. Eventually when the time comes to take a bigger leap, you'll have run out of excuses and you'll be surprised what you can accomplish or things you'll experience. Soon after you'll wonder why you didn't leap sooner.

2. Trust that once you leap you will fly, or a net will appear. We always feel like we can't take a leap unless the timing is right and if it "makes sense." Like waiting until we have the money, waiting until the kids are grown, or waiting until you've researched enough. But life doesn't work that way. It is only when we "jump" that we know.

3. If you're keeping your aspirations hidden in your head, take a chance, unlock them, and share. Reach out to your support network. Be vulnerable and share your feelings. Friends or a mentor can be an incredible source of encouragement to just go for it!

Glow Girl Affirmation:
I go beyond barriers to possibilities.

11

Glow Together

"Alone we can do so little; together we can do so much."

—*Helen Keller*

T TAKES A village. Not to just raise children, but to rise to our best selves as women. I don't know where I would be without my girlfriends. They have been by my side, supporting me and cheering me on. Throughout my personal and entrepreneurial journey, the women in my life gave me the fuel to keep going through many challenges. I call them glow-getters!

In that first year of creating my beverage brand, I had a circle of friends. Unknowingly, we created our own tribe. We would get together monthly to collaborate and share our ideas (and cocktails, of course!). We would offer our opinions, advice, and encouragement to one another. Every friend in my tribe contributed to my success and they listened to me when I was hurting, cried with me, and celebrated my victories with me.

I love this concept: behind every successful woman is a tribe of other successful women who have her back.

We need to surround ourselves with people that push us to do better. People who motivate us and give off positive energy and lift us up. *#glowgetters*

In our technology-driven world, we can easily surround ourselves with inspiring people online. And it's so easy to connect with someone with a quick "like", "follow" or emoji. It only takes a second.

While having technology at our fingertips makes it extremely easy to connect with others, we all spend so much time online that it's so easy for us to feel disconnected, isolated, and alone in the real world.

Connecting online with the swipe of a finger is not a human connection.

Real, authentic relationships are not as easy or as simple as a "swipe" or a "like." They take vulnerability, forgiveness, and openness, but they also give you a connection that accelerates your goals, gives you true support, lifts you up, and inspires you to keep going.

We can have hundreds of Facebook friends and Instagram followers, but how many people in your life are you *truly* connected to? Like when you're having the worst day ever, feeling like you can't get motivated and feel lonely or sad. Is there someone you can reach out to who will be there to lift you up? To tell you, *you got this girl.* To tell you that tomorrow will be a better day. To tell you how special you are and to hang in there.

The years I felt isolated it was extremely hard for me to reach out and tell my friends how I was feeling. I didn't want to burden them and frankly, I thought it would be easier to just wallow in self-pity, cry it out, zone out watching a movie, eat some ice cream, and then try to ignore how I was feeling. I thought no one would want to hear about my sad life.

Well, sister, I'm here to tell you, once you let yourself be vulnerable many things start to happen. Once you start sharing, you realize you are not alone. You realize that the deep sadness you're feeling while you think everyone is living their best life is actually not true. The women in your life who are there for you and "get you" are the women you need to lean on. They are the women who are in *your* tribe.

When you support yourself with people who bring out your best, you can do more, be more, and ultimately give more.

Without my tribe of glow-getters, I certainly would not be where I am today, having built a successful beverage business and now continuing to grow and evolve in my purpose and mission and sharing my life with vulnerability on these pages.

Let yourself be seen. Vulnerability is the way back to each other so don't be afraid to walk along that path.

Some of you might be thinking, *I can do it all myself. I'm smart and capable. After all, I've already gotten this far.* It's possible, but the truth is we need each other to flourish. We need a tribe to surround us on our journey to greatness.

There was a time not long ago that I thought I could do it all on my own. I think there was something inside me that wanted to prove to myself that I could. I had lots of experience in handling life's challenges. I didn't need anyone to help me. Once I began to go to therapy, I realized how I was isolating myself.

If I truly wanted to grow, not just my business but myself personally, I would need to start to put myself out there. I wanted people to know my story, but it was all new to me. I had my core group of friends, but to put myself out there to strangers or people in the business world was scary.

I finally realized, especially after breaking away from the co-dependency of my marriage, that I needed and wanted to connect with like-minded people. I wanted to share experiences both good and bad and grow. Gradually it happened, year after year, as I began to put myself out there even if I risked rejection.

After my parents' divorce, my mom and I moved twice in two years, so I was in three different schools in three years until she re-married. The apartment building we moved to in third grade was huge and overwhelming to me. The school was too. I didn't know anyone, and my mom was continually encouraging me to make friends, but it was difficult for me. I was fine just hanging out with her at home.

One day, she told me to go out to the community playground, all by myself. "Don't come back until you make one friend," she said. I remember crying, hysterically sobbing, all the way there. I felt like I was walking the plank to my death. Thankfully, I eventually ended up making a friend who lived in the apartments and I was so proud of myself for accomplishing it, despite the fact I was terrified.

When I first created the idea of Sipp I believed in my beverage, but I'm not so sure I believed in myself. There were many times I had to travel to events by myself and I was petrified. I felt like I was that little girl walking into the playground. I wondered who would talk to me. What did I have to offer? Would they like me?

I remember standing in the middle of the room at a conference, surrounded by hundreds of people and everyone seemed to know everyone. And there I was in the middle of the room, solo and scared. I wanted to run to the restroom and hide.

But instead, I took baby steps. It's amazing now how far I've come when I look back—and it didn't come easy. It was taking that first leap of faith to talk to someone I didn't know and hope they didn't go running in the other direction. Once I took a chance and saw I was still alive, it became easier and easier.

Finally, I was just myself and people liked me—the real me. The more times I ventured out to a conference or event, it got easier and I came out of my shell. It's like my social butterfly was waiting to get out.

Little did I know, as I was building my business, I was also building my self-confidence.

Fast forward to now, I have very close friends and am extremely blessed. Looking back ten years ago, I would have never guessed this was going to be my path after so many years of feeling isolated. Through the strength of community, taking risks, and putting myself out there, I made friends who became my biggest supporters and supporters who became wonderful friends. Friends who encouraged me along my journey.

There are friends in life and friends for life.

Our journey as a woman is difficult at times. We are juggling so many things and somehow everyone expects us to handle it. Like Superwoman. Think about the things you were tasked within just this past week. If you have a job, then you have your work responsibilities. If you're a mom then you have parent responsibilities, dropping kids off at school, extracurricular activities, projects, maybe even a bake sale. Then you add grocery shopping, cooking, cleaning, handling repairs that come up, and oh and what about that birthday card you need to get for a friend, the dress you need to find for a party, or that thing you volunteered for.

There always seems to be something and it's up to us to manage it all. And if we want to create a side hustle or a business then we have to somehow weave that into our everyday demands. I know it's overwhelming because I've been there. There aren't enough hours in the day. But for me, there was always this drive to create something bigger than where I was at. And to do that I knew I needed to put in the time to make it happen. I had to somehow squeeze more hours in each day to create my dream.

The good news is because we are such stellar multitaskers as women, we can do it. And there are days where you don't know how you can fit it all in, and there will be days where you wonder why you're working on your side hustle when you have everything else in your life going on and children who demand your time, but sister, if you have this passion burning inside of you, you have to follow it.

So, on those days when you're feeling overwhelmed or

wonder if what you're doing is even worth it in the long run, that's when you need to stop for a moment and turn to your tribe of glow-getters. That's when you need to reach out and tell someone how your struggling. The tribe will be there for you and you'll be there for the tribe. And the one thing that I've learned is that on the days that I'm down and feeling like I can't go on; those are the days that someone else in my tribe is feeling upbeat and can lift me up, support me, and be my cheerleader. And then on the days when I'm feeling upbeat, someone in my tribe needs me to lift them up. That's how it all works! If we truly want to rise to our best life, we absolutely cannot do it alone.

I love the saying, "If you are the smartest person in a room then you are in the wrong room." In order to grow, it is important to place yourself in the company of people who are living the kind of life you want. Listen to podcasts; read books and blogs. Keep on learning and don't stop. Become passionate about your pursuit of knowledge. And if you want to continue to grow, you will need a community of individuals who believe in you and sincerely want you to succeed.

The people you hang out with will either fuel your self-doubt or fuel your self-confidence. When you allow the wrong people in your house things come up missing. Things like joy, faith, love, laughter, and peace.

Take a look at the people you have in your life. Who do you tend to spend the most time with? Who was really there for you when you needed someone? Who was just using you for connections or only wants you to listen to them?

If you want to be successful, then surround yourself with successful people.

If you want to be positive and happy then surround yourself with happy upbeat people.

We become like the people we spend time with.

What Jim Rohn says is so true, "You are the average of the five people you spend the most time with."

Take a moment to reflect on the following: *Who are the people you spend the most time with? Do they lift you up or bring you down? Are they proactive glow-getters exhibiting qualities that you admire or people who just complain?*

Stay away from "still" people. People who are still unhappy, still complaining, still miserable, still nowhere.

And if there are friends who you think should be in your life and you have to continuously chase them, stop. They should be chasing after you. It's mentally exhausting and do you want to waste your energy like that? (This applies to men too if you happen to be in the dating world!)

A friend recently shared this quote with me: Stop being the one to text first and you'll see how many dead plants you were watering. Boom!

Know the people that are meant to come into your life will.

It's remarkable that when you put yourself out there, the right people will show up. I've had the most wonderful people give time and advice selflessly because they wanted to see me succeed. Those are the people that you want to spend your time with.

What's the opposite of a glow-getter? A dimmer. Beware of dimmers. These are people who say your dreams are too big. And if someone tells you your dream is too big, then tell them they think too small.

Don't dim your glow to match the people around you. You will meet people who refuse to see your glow because they haven't found theirs.

You can't be positive when you are surrounded by negativity. And if you have those people in your life who doubt that you can do that great new idea you came up with, they are probably scared that you will! Don't let the haters get you down. Tell them to put down that glass of Hater-ade! Move on. You are better than that. You're reading this book because you want something more out of your life.

Stick with the people who pull the magic out of you and not the madness.

Surrounding ourselves with the right women makes all the difference in our personal growth and overall happiness. I know the difference between feeling isolated and alone and having beautiful, supportive and encouraging women in my life. As women, we need to be there for each other. It's not so easy in a world of social media when we struggle with comparisonitis.

We should be building each other up and not tearing each other down. It only diminishes our influence and impact.

Spending time with positive-minded people who are building their dreams will have an impact on your thinking and consequently your actions. A tribe means more minds, more experience, and more resources.

Hang out with people who fit your future not your history.

Here's a great quote from Robin Sharma: "Associate only with positive, focused people who you can learn from and who will not drain your valuable energy with uninspiring attitudes. By developing relationships with those committed to constant improvement and the pursuit of the best that life has to offer, you will have plenty of company on your path to the top of whatever mountain you seek to climb."

Identify who the glow-getters are in your life and create your own Glow Together Tribe! Try to create a good balance. You don't want to feel like you are not where you should be because everyone in your tribe is so further along and vice-versa—you don't want to be the one always helping others to grow.

Be open-minded. A supportive tribe of women is a combination of all different women from different backgrounds and stories. Often the best women to be a part of your tribe are opposite of you in many ways so you can all learn from each other and see things from a unique perspective.

I found while I'm good at lifting up and encouraging women in my tribe, it's challenging to see the things I see in them within myself. And they experience the same. They find it easy to tell me how great they think I am and point out all my accomplishments, but they have a hard time lifting themselves up. That's *exactly* why we need each other. Our sisters are like a spectacular, powerful mirror. They reflect back to us what we can't see, but what *they* can see. If we can find all these magnificent qualities in them, then we should be able to find them within ourselves. The reality is that what we see in them, we also have within us, but sometimes we can't see it or don't believe it.

They sing the words to our song when we forget them.

As women, while we think we can handle it all ourselves, deep down we crave the connection and feeling of belonging that can only come from sisterhood.

When we connect with women, we connect with ourselves. I've seen it and I've felt it. Going to a women's conference is such an incredible experience. Being in a group of women from all different backgrounds sharing and learning from one another is an experience like no other. It's empowering and freeing. Opening up and sharing things that are personal in nature takes great courage especially with women you don't know. But once you share with vulnerability, it creates a deep connection that we crave and need.

Don't hold back. Being honest is a critical component to creating a successful tribe. We may not feel comfortable expressing how we truly feel in fear of embarrassing ourselves or protecting others. But the more you share with open honesty and transparency, the more you will be establishing a foundation of trust. We are all in this together, sister!

And when we feel we are in a trusting, supportive tribe

we tend to be willing to take more risks because if we face rejection the impact won't be as brutal because we have our tribe to cushion our fall. We know that they love and accept us no matter what.

We all need multiple soul-connecting relationships for every aspect of our life in order to elevate ourselves to live our best life. When I was a teen, my youth church group was the light of my life, especially in the darkness of feeling alone.

We went on weekend retreats and did all night dance-a-thon fundraisers. The one big summer excursion we had planned was a bike trek from the beginning of Cape Cod to the tip and back all in one week. I like to ride my bike now and then, and my biggest bike "trek" was maybe to my friend's house in an adjacent neighborhood or to the 7-Eleven convenience store at the bottom of my street to occasionally pick up some donuts.

Despite the unknown of what this trek would entail, I knew I wanted to be a part of it. I felt different with my youth group than at any other time. I felt part of something bigger. Something positive and uplifting. The pastor who ran the youth group was one of the kindest, funniest. inspiring man I had known. He made me want to be better. He made me feel safe. He created a tribe and we were all leaders. He showed us that on our trip through Cape Cod. There were fourteen of us and it was quite the sight, seeing us all in a row on our bikes.

The first day after we were dropped off, we biked forty miles. This was a challenge for most of us, but some who were more experienced bikers could go much faster and ahead of us, but they didn't. They went behind us and in the middle of us cheering us on and encouraging us to keep going. And when one of us fell, yes it happened many times, we all stopped and helped.

Every day that entire week, we biked on average thirty to forty miles. We were exhausted but we were a team. We held each other up when one of us was down and we celebrated our accomplishment together at the end of every day. This experience bonded us. There were no cell phones then, so we were truly "together." As each day passed, I felt stronger and stronger. And it was partly because I impressed myself that I could bike the number miles I did (butt blisters and all!), but also from the support from every person in my youth group. Those last few days were so rough. We were all tired, but we were on a mission to finish where we started one week later— and we did. It was such a tremendous accomplishment for each and everyone one of us. I never experienced camaraderie and encouragement like that. This trip showed me the power of a tribe and I was forever changed.

Surround yourself with a tribe of women who are confident and secure enough to know that there's room for all of you to make it to the finish line.

Tribes have been around forever. Whether it's spiritual tribes or community tribes the common goal was to connect to each other and share ideas. In the old model, there was typically a tribe leader. This isn't about being in a clique reminiscent of high-school or being the leader of an exclusive club. In the new model, there are many leaders who create an empowering circle of support to encourage one another to follow our purpose. That's what makes a Glow Together Tribe.

I love this quote from Phylicia Rashad: "Any time women come together with a collective intention, it's a powerful thing. Whether it's sitting down making a quilt, in a kitchen preparing a meal, in a club reading the same book, or around the table playing cards, or planning a birthday party, when women come together with a collective intention, magic happens."

Being heard, being supported, discovering that you're not alone unlocks something inside us, and we can see and feel the power of what we can truly accomplish. We are reminded who we are and realize that we are not alone.

We all share the same struggles and insecurities. We all doubt ourselves and are critical of ourselves inside and out. But recognize we are all still standing despite our struggles and acknowledge what life-changing things we are capable of individually and collectively. We support one another and stand strong in our lives and in our businesses.

And know that by surrounding ourselves with strong women doesn't diminish our impact or what we seek to accomplish, but rather it multiplies and strengthens it. You are creating a community of support, love, and trust. This isn't about being lazy because we feel we can't do it on our own. It's about camaraderie, cultivating, and choosing to be a part of a powerful community that is creating a positive impact due to the collective effort of the tribe.

You love and value yourself enough to be a part of a tribe of women who you support, and they support you to rise to your greatness. We all have our own unique gifts to share so let's support each other and shine!

A woman with a vision empowers an empire of women to do more, see more, and be more.

By "glowing" together we can help build a better world.

A few of my favorite tips on how to glow together...

1. Create a Glow Together Tribe: Invite between two and five friends to join you in your home, coffee shop, or place of choice. Let them know you want to create a tribe of empowered women. Plan to meet for a couple of hours depending on the number of women.

   Start off by checking in with each other. Each member can share how they are doing and feeling. When each woman shares, everyone else listens supportively. Having the experience of being heard and supported with undivided attention is what we all desire.

Next, share the challenges personally or professionally you are each facing and then give a little time to offer support. Then, share something positive that recently happened. Something little or big to celebrate. Acknowledge each woman's accomplishment. Lastly, set a goal or intention you would like to commit to before the next meet-up. One action that moves you forward in a positive direction. As you all share you will form a powerful bond.

2. Find an accountability partner. When we are starting out growing our business, it can feel isolating as a solo-preneur and we have to continually be the one to push and motivate ourselves. Our busy lives can tend to take over and keep us from pursuing a goal or dream. We can then put it off due to more pressing issues. My solution to ensure we are meeting the goals we set for ourselves is an accountability partner. This could be someone in your tribe or if you don't have a tribe yet, connect with a supportive friend who is in a similar situation trying to hustle and grow a business.

I do this with a friend now and it is genius. This is a way to reflect on our priorities, outline our goals, and offer each other accountability as well as ideas. We also celebrate the wins! Here's what we do:

a. Write and email our weekly goals to each other by Monday morning.

b. Have a mid-week check-in. Text or call.

c. Write and email our accomplishments for the week to each other by Friday and have a check-in call at 4 p.m.

Rinse and repeat every week!

3. I highly recommend the book, *Tribes* by Seth Godin. It's one of the best books I've read on tribes and community. He also has a TED Talk on YouTube.

Seth believes that each and every one of us has the opportunity to make a massive change in the world and create a movement by bringing together like-minded people.

Glow Girl Affirmation:
I choose to be friends
with like-minded people.

12

Mirror, Mirror

"Smile in the mirror. Do that every morning and you'll start to see a big difference in your life."

—*Yoko Ono*

IRROR, MIRROR ON the wall, who's the fairest of them all? You are. And you are enough.

Why is it when we look in the mirror, we often criticize the woman looking back at us?

When you look in the mirror, what does that little voice inside your head say?

Like the fairy tales, what if we had a mirror to tell us how beautiful we are every day? Beautiful like a princess. And maybe tell us we can even have a handsome prince or princess or snuggle buddy or partner in crime…and live happily ever after.

In the past, I don't think I can ever recall looking in the mirror and thinking about my happily ever after. It was more like a happily *never* after.

Mirror, mirror on the wall…*what the hell happened?*

After my mom's divorce to my stepfather when I was fourteen things really changed for me. While living in the home with him was at times scary, I loved my school, my neighborhood, our home, and I also loved that we had a family. We left because he was physically abusive to me. He slammed me down on the floor and that was the straw that broke the camel's back for my mom. She wasn't having it anymore.

Despite what was happening it was the closest version I had of a true "family." When that fell apart, I was relieved to not have my abusive and angry stepfather in my life, but then there was another side of me that was sad to not be part of a family anymore. My stepbrother who I had become very close with, as well as my stepsisters, would no longer be a part of my life. The home in the idyllic neighborhood where I could go up or down the street and hang out with friends was no longer our home. When we left, everything was unknown and in a backward way, I felt like it was my fault because if he didn't hit *me*, we would most likely still be there.

My mom was able to find an apartment in the same town so I could continue in the same school system. I was glad to still have that connection. But even despite still having that, we moved to the other side of town in an apartment which was quite different than where we had been living. But the biggest unexpected change was the "family" lifestyle I knew was gone. Being a teenager at a time when so many things were changing for me, it was pretty scary. I felt so alone, and I struggled. In many ways, the other side of town felt like the other side of the world.

I began to battle with depression and didn't really have the tools to know what to do. Everything was changing around me, and I was trying to adapt the best I could. My mom's newfound freedom caused her to be out more than she had been when we were in "family." Because she was married so young and then subsequently married shortly after the divorce with my dad, I could see that now this was her single time. And while I could logically see that and understand it, it was incredibly difficult for me because I was in my formidable teen years. I felt all alone and with my bio-dad adjusting to my teen transition as well, things were becoming a little rocky with us.

I felt so much pain, and even though people would tell me how beautiful I was—I just couldn't see it. I didn't know how to fill this huge gaping dark hole I felt inside of me. A void so massive that no matter what I did, it always felt like it would never leave. My mom was dating now, and I wasn't really sure how to handle that. She was the mom who had dinner on the table at six every night because that's what my stepfather wanted.

This whole new life was different and scary. As I was trying to find my way, I began to search for ways to fill this sad, empty void. I had lots of attention from men and I used that to feed my ego. Every time I found myself in the arms of a man, I thought it would give me what I needed. But it was always a temporary "fix" and never truly worked. I ended up feeling more and more hollow over and over again. Nothing I did helped me find the answer.

There were periods of time that helped pull me through. My best friend who was always there for me, my high school guidance counselor, and my church youth group. These things kept me grounded and feeling like maybe there was hope for me.

On the other dark side, there were so many moments of me feeling like I didn't even know how I was going to continue on. I never felt like I was enough. That I would never be enough for anyone.

I remember one night feeling so sad and alone and walking to a bus stop shelter a couple of miles from our apartment in the middle of farm country. I didn't even know where I was going or what I was doing. I sat in that bus shelter in the pouring down rain for hours. It was a brown metal frame with a glass shell. I never really understood why it was there because I never saw any buses. And all I wanted to do was go anywhere. Anywhere but where I was. But instead, I sat there on the cold metal bench with legs tucked into my chest and my arms hugging them close to me shivering. I cried like I never cried before.

I knew at that point I was at my lowest. I remember feeling so deeply alone, feeling like no one understood me. I had no idea how I was going to crawl out of the dark isolated space that I somehow managed to find myself in.

As cars drove by flashes of headlights would catch the glistening rain streaming down the glass walls. It was almost if I was surrounded in tears and I wondered if anybody would see me through all the tears. I felt invisible. *No one sees me for who I am—my true self,* I thought. *How could I ever be enough when no one even sees me.* Was I not lovable?

Hours and hours went by and I remember feeling like I could stay in this bus shelter forever and no one would even know. No one would care where I was.

With tears continuing to stream down my face as fast as the rain was streaming down the glass shell that was protecting me from the elements, I felt broken and like *no one* could protect me, not even this shelter.

Eventually, as the sun was beginning to rise, I saw a glimmer of light. A glimmer of hope. The tiniest beam of light was breaking through the darkness and a tiny flicker of hope glowing inside me said, "I am enough," even despite all my flaws.

I had the realization; there wasn't any bus that could take me out of the darkness. No bus to take me where I wanted to go. I thought, *I could continue to stay here and go nowhere or go back and face my life.* It was my choice. I knew the only way I could get to where I wanted to go was to go back.

Even despite the deep loneliness I was feeling, at that moment something shifted. That little flicker of light refused to go out. It was up to me from that point forward to keep the flame going. I knew that no one could tell me that I am enough except for myself.

I came across this quote from Erin Van Vuren and it resonated with me when I think of this time in my life. "I will not be another flower, picked for my beauty and left to die. I will be wild, difficult to find, and impossible to forget."

When I looked back at my younger self, when things were simple and I had joy in my heart and aspirations to fly, I couldn't figure out where she went. I just knew that she needed saving and I had to bring her back. I knew that if I didn't do it, that nobody else would. I was the only one that could save myself. And when I finally realized that it was up to me, then I knew I had to stop the hurtful despicable things that I had been telling myself. The only way I could bring myself back was to nurture myself and love myself like no one has ever loved me. I needed to tell myself that I am beautiful just the way I am. And I am not stupid, but that I am resilient. If I make a mistake, then I learn from that mistake. To stop thinking that life was just happening to me and I had no control. To know that I am strong enough to create my own path in life. To forge forward on my path with confidence. To stop letting things happen to me and to let myself happen to life.

Don't abandon yourself. The journey to self-love isn't easy and it's a process. But I can tell you it's totally worth the effort. For us to rise to the greatest versions of ourselves we must start from a strong, loving, solid foundation of self-worth.

Why do we speak to ourselves from our pain and not our power?

It amazes me how many I women I know who don't see the beauty in themselves. How many women who don't see what they have to offer and how many don't value themselves.

Why don't we feel good enough, despite all that we do at home, for our family, and in our work? Could it be the images of perfection we are bombarded with in media, the expectation to be perfect from the past we still carry with us, or trauma we experienced? Despite all our accomplishments we still continue to struggle with this. And low self-esteem is more than not feeling beautiful, it's the feeling of not being good enough or not worthy, which is the deeper issue.

So many of us experience this. It saddens me when I think about how many beautiful, fierce women don't follow through on things simply because they don't feel they're good enough, pretty enough, smart enough, confident enough, courageous enough, or anything enough.

You all know now that I was there too. Right alongside you, allowing these things to hold me back. And it wasn't until I started to believe in myself; little by little, it continually reinforced that I *am* good enough; that things began to shift.

The first step to accepting your greatness is to own your past and recognize your negative thoughts as the untruths that they are. Like pulling back the curtain on "The Wizard of Oz," and exposing him as a fraud; we can expose the lies that we tell ourselves and strip them of their power.

So instead of letting our fears and false beliefs aimlessly steer our ship, *we* become the captain and guide it out of the darkness and into the light.

Honestly, it's still something I continue to work on even now as I'm writing this chapter. When I had this overwhelming desire to write this book, my initial thought was, *who am I to advise other people? Who would want to read to* my *stories?* Even despite women continually telling me how much I have to offer. That's a perfect example of how deep this can go and if you don't start working on this right now, it's not going to change.

Negative thoughts only have the power we allow them to have.

Let go of striving for perfection and accept your true identity. You are incredibly complex, and your physical appearance is only one facet of who you are. If you fixate on your imperfections and downplay other aspects, you then overlook the wholeness of who you are.

I read something once that suggested we view ourselves as a magnificent painting. When you look close up at a painting you see abstract brushstrokes that may not be lovely looking at them individually, but if you step back you will see how all those brushstrokes that uniquely make their own mark, actually create and wholly encompass the beauty of the painting.

Work on seeing yourself as that valuable one-of-a-kind painting, full of unique brushstrokes. You are a masterpiece.

One day my mirror told me I shouldn't go to a party because it said I looked fat in my outfit (and may have also been directing some very offensive "yo momma" jokes at me). The mirror laughed at me and told me I would feel self-conscious all night. I listened and I stayed home. The next time my mirror told me that I should stay home, I turned my back to it and went anyway. Do you know what happened? A woman at the party complimented me saying I have the most beautiful hair she'd ever seen and then continued to share how she just couldn't get her hair to look right that night and almost didn't come. Boom! We are all in it together sister! Don't let it hold you back.

Your mirror will tell you that you have tummy fat but won't tell you, "that's okay because you had a baby." Your mirror will tell you that your pants are too tight but won't say, "that's okay because you just bought a smaller size since you're working out." Your mirror will point out that scar on your face but won't thank you for removing something that could've been melanoma and possibly you saved your life. We *need* to tell our mirror to go find a new job!

In reflecting back over the past decade, I can see the journey of my transformation. The journey has not been an easy one, but to have hope again is a feeling that has breathed new life into me. To look in the mirror and know that I am enough.

To know that I deserve the best. To know that I now have a purpose to share my message.

By being vulnerable, sharing all my struggles and all the times that I felt broken inside, I want you all to know that you can come through whatever challenges you are facing. I'm not talking about covering ourselves up from the outside, but to find the light inside of us. To glow from the inside out. To glow from the core of your being. So that no matter what is on the outside, it doesn't matter. What matters is the inside.

Work on being in love with the person in the mirror who has gone through so much and is still standing.

You are enough does not mean that you've reached some magical pinnacle and that you are finished growing and changing and learning. This isn't about being perfect. It doesn't mean that you are self-sufficient and don't need anyone because you are enough. It means you understand that you do need people and that's okay. When you are enough it's easier to ask for help because you know that your challenges and imperfections are not a reflection of your self-worth. When we value our self-worth then we know the value of getting help. We are worth it.

We are not flawless and yes, we will make mistakes, but we own them. Some unfortunate things might have happened to us in the past, but we accept them. We welcome them because they are a part of us, and they will help us learn and grow. Not every decision we make may be the best one but celebrate the smart choices and learn from your missteps.

When we accept our imperfections, we discover our perfection, strengths, and gifts within us.

And you don't need to strive to be more worthy or lovable or try to prove yourself to anyone. It's not about changing yourself—it's about being yourself. It's about loving yourself for the beautiful messy woman that you are who shows up every day for herself.

No more judging, only loving. This is a transformation and it will take time. Be patient with yourself and love yourself. Unconditionally accept yourself as you are.

We can all look in the mirror and cover our faces with fancy expensive makeup and while we may look glowing on the outside, the inside is still filled with sadness. No matter what kind of makeup you apply, it will never mask the pain from the inside.

If we truly don't believe we deserve a big, beautiful joy-filled life, I can tell you sister, it will never happen, no matter what we try to do to feel love or loved.

The root of many of our behaviors like compulsive shopping, overeating, and excessive drinking is that we don't feel like we are enough, therefore we are trying to continually fill a void, a bottomless pit that never can be filled with external things.

Are any of you out there using behaviors like these to comfort yourself; to mask the pain of not feeling like you are enough?

Well, let me tell you sister, I've been there too. And it never works. The drink that I felt I "needed" to calm me or make me more lovable or funny, the dessert I "needed" to make me feel better after a bad day, or the clothes I "needed" to make me look thinner. All of these things never filled my emptiness.

When we are faced with challenges, it's not always easy to stay strong with the idea, "I am enough." But today is a new day. The greatest power we have in life is the power to choose. I'm here to tell you that you have the power to change your inner voice of self-doubt and change what you tell yourself when you look in the mirror.

Adam Roa, a brilliant poet who inspires me, beautifully said, "Take a good long look in the mirror and say, I am who I've been looking for." I love this quote because it embodies the thought that we need to love ourselves first.

I'm going to ask you when you look at yourself in the mirror to not just look "at" yourself, but to look "in" yourself. I'm asking you to look past your make-up. Look into your eyes and see what you find.

Say out loud. "I am enough." How did it feel? Does it feel authentic? Do you immediately add on "buts" or "ifs" after you say it?

Today is the day I'm standing up for you, my sisters.

Let's start with believing and owning that "I am enough."

You can "change your mind." I'm even going to hashtag it!! #changeyourmind

There may be some days where you need more to pull yourself out of darkness. You know those days where you feel like nothing seems to be going right. Those days when you're doubting your path or someone says something cruel to you. You look in the mirror and see tears welling up in your eyes. If you have self-doubt creeping in, especially on bad days, then you need to develop a self-mantra and read it back to yourself. Creating a mantra is something personal. I suggest you create one so that you are armed with it on the dark days.

After you told yourself you are enough, what popped into your mind? Write these things down and they will be part of creating your personal mantra. You need to counter them with positive declarations. Make it specific. Not general statements like: I am worthy, I am funny, I am talented—all of which I'm sure you are, but this about *you*. The core of you.

Here is an example of my mantra:

I am full of life and light. I see the positive in negatives. People love my laugh and I make people smile. I am adventurous and love to take risks. I sparkle. I am loyal. I'm a loving mom. I am a hard worker and will do everything in my power to inspire others. I am an artist. I am full of empathy and compassion and genuinely want to make the world a better place. I'm always learning. I empower women. I make mistakes, but I learn from them. I am going deeper than I've ever been to look for answers, to feel like I've never felt, to learn, to connect, to seek the truth, to discover, to be open-minded, to experience miracles and serendipity, to believe. I am enough.

The most important relationship we will ever have in life is the one with ourselves. Think about that for a moment. The *most* important relationship. Don't you want that to be the best that it can?

Forgive yourself for placing all those critical and judgmental thoughts on yourself and realize that today, this is a miracle and a gift of a day—a fresh start.

In the words of poet Adam Roa, "Treat yourself like someone you loved."

I've embraced the bad things that happened to me in the past. They made me who I am today. I now look at those things from my past as gifts. I've learned to thank them for making me who I am today. To empower myself. To be proud of myself that I pulled myself out of the darkness and began to look at things in a different light. To be open-minded to different perspectives. To take the morsels of learning that were being given to me and embrace them. To interject these new learnings and perspectives in my life to open the door from the dark prison I was living in inside my mind. And crack by crack, seeing more and more light as each new perspective I embraced, each self-affirmation I gave myself, each self-limiting barrier I broke through, each new accomplishment, each new obstacle I overcame—all led me to the place where I now embrace my greatness and say, "I am enough."

By sharing my journey back to the light, I want every woman to see that they deserve to be in the light too. It's time for us to come out of the darkness and show our spectacular, beautiful, wonderful selves—and be proud of who we are.

It truly breaks my heart that so many of us still don't

celebrate our beauty and at the same time, it also fires me up to continue on my journey, spreading my message and stories.

The more you tell yourself *you are enough*, the more you'll believe it. I know it sounds simplistic, but your self-love will begin to fill the emptiness.

So, commit to yourself, believe it will work, listen to your affirmations, and make it a habit.

"I am enough, just as I am, right at this very moment."

Speaking your self-affirmations out loud in front of the mirror looking while into your own eyes sends the subconscious message that you are there for you and you are important. When you make this commitment on a daily basis you will begin to see a change in how you feel. It seems too simple to make a difference, but it will change your life.

Look in the mirror now and tell yourself that you are still standing despite all the challenges you have gone through and you are enough—just as you were made to be.

I am here, standing right next to you, sister, and I believe that you are enough. Just as you are, right at this very moment. Yes, some of you may have been told or may believe that you're too big, too small, too old, too young, too brown, too light, too fat, too thin, too pretty, too ugly, too…anything to ever be "enough." No, sister. You are *more* than enough. The accolades, the car, the trophy spouse, the perfect house—that is all extra. You were and are enough just for showing up—beautiful, caring, unique *you*.

A few of my favorite tips to help you cultivate the belief that you are enough…

1. I highly recommend checking out Adam Roa. His quotes included in this chapter are from his poem, "You are Who You've Been Looking For." You *must* see the video where he recites this poem. #Love!

2. Embrace a *simple* mirror mantra. Use lipstick or a sticky note and leave yourself an inspirational quote or words of encouragement. After your shower or while putting on your makeup, repeat the encouraging words to yourself. For example: "Hello beautiful," "Today is going to rock," or "You glow, girl!" (of course!)

3. Take my *I AM ENOUGH* Challenge. Stand in front of a mirror, look into your eyes, and repeat the following out loud with conviction once a day for a month (even if you don't believe it at first—#FakeItTillYouMakeIt). It might feel a little odd at first talking to yourself in the mirror but push through the uncomfortableness because in the end, it will all be worth it.

I am **ENOUGH**

I am **STRONG**

I am **BRAVE**

I am **BEAUTIFUL**

TODAY will be **AMAZING**

I am **ENOUGH**

You will begin to create a new narrative and create your new story.

Glow Girl Affirmation:
I am enough. I have always been enough.
And I will always be enough.

13

Hustle & Heart

"My personal belief is that business can be fun, it can be conducted with love and a powerful force for good."

—*Anita Roddick*

WE HAVE TO follow our heart in everything we do. Do you know what sets your heart on fire; that feeling of passion that glows bright inside you?

Maybe you know what that is and wake up every day hustling with passion but are struggling to make the impact you desire. Or maybe you've lost sight of what it was that brought you joy, what you set out to accomplish because life got in the way or expectations of others swayed you in another direction.

Most of us were taught how to be successful the traditional way—go to college and get a good stable job, but we are not taught how to be fulfilled and live our lives in alignment with who we are, and what we truly want. What we feel in our hearts. And as a result, we may end up doing what we think we're *supposed* to do and sometimes even fulfilling someone else's definition of success based on their expectations.

My dad worked for the same company for thirty-five years. He loved his job and what he did. He was a brilliant engineer and worked experimenting with lasers. It was a great company and provided stability. In his mind this was "success." I remember going to his workplace every year on, "take your child to work day." I absolutely loved it. I saw him in his element, and he looked so smart. It was clear his colleagues looked up to him and I was so proud to call him my dad.

His wish for me upon graduating college was to find a good stable job, just like him. One that offered advancement, a good salary, and a 401(k) plan. Stability. While, I knew this was what he wanted for me, I just couldn't wrap my head around it. To me it sounded so normal and unfulfilling...aka boring. I was definitely not my father's daughter in that regard.

In my first year at college, I was just going through the motions. It didn't help that I was going to a satellite branch of the school so most of the students were older and it wasn't the "college" experience I was hoping for (think the show *Community* set in rural Connecticut without the cross-dressing Dean Pelton). And since I didn't go to college for art, I wasn't feeling very inspired.

My creative entrepreneurial spirit was buried deep down inside and was scratching and clawing to get out. Because of what I knew was expected of me, I ignored the voices. I ignored them even when I felt something different in my heart. That was until one day as I was flipping through *Entrepreneur* magazine. I read this magazine regularly, but something on this particular day inspired me to make a life changing decision. I was going to start a business. I had no idea what business, but I knew that this was what I was meant to do, despite what was "expected" of me. I was meant to be an entrepreneur and use my creative abilities.

I researched all types of businesses and since I was only eighteen, I thought it might be a good idea to buy into a franchise, because it would give me the foundation to start a proven business concept. After much research I came across a video store franchise. Videos were hot, I thought (I'm dating myself here...but who remembers making it a "Blockbuster Night?").

I drove three states away to the franchise corporate office and met with the owner and other people on the team. I know they were skeptical because of my age but I'm pretty sure I won them over with my passion. After the meeting, I left armed with a thick stack of papers that included everything I would need to open a video store and also included a super extensive franchise agreement. I remember reading it through and wondering what I was getting myself into.

Shortly after our meeting they notified me that I was accepted into the franchise program and at that point I would need to raise the capital needed for the franchise fee and all the costs to open the store...you know just a *small* feat.

I went to the library and took out a bunch of books on business plans. While I was working on the business plan, I also met with real estate agents to look at potential retail locations for the store. Once I finally found a location that I thought could be a successful spot, I finished my business plan and made the bold decision to present it to the head of a local bank in the town that I was looking to open the store. I had read in one of the business books that this could be a successful way to get a loan because the local banks encouraged small businesses in their community. Those were the days...not to mention phones attached to the wall, beepers, and waiting a week to watch your favorite television show!

So, there I went, nervous and all of eighteen-years-old walking into a bank with my new spiffy suit and shiny leather briefcase, that I just purchased the day before to look "professional." I told the women who greeted me that I had an appointment with the president. She said I must be mistaken. He only meets with people regarding loans and after I had to convince her I veritably did have an appointment and that no,

I wasn't applying for the part-time teller position, she reluctantly led me to his office.

I sat on the other side of the bank president's large desk behind closed doors and presented my business plan and explained how I would build a successful business in their community. He asked me where I was currently working, and I told him that I was in college. He asked if I had ever owned a business before and I told him no, but that I have always had an entrepreneurial spirit. I had also worked since I was fifteen and managed a retail store at sixteen. He asked me if he were to give me the $60,000 that I was asking for, what would I spend it on. I told him I had everything outlined in my business plan. He reviewed it and by his facial expression (eyebrow raises) he looked impressed. Then as he closed the last page on my plan, he asked me the biggest question of all. Why did I think that I would be a successful business owner? I thought, *wow, I came prepared with all my facts. Everything I have garnered from the franchise company, all the tips and suggestions in my business books, my stellar business plan that outlined every detail.* But the one thing that none of those things covered was: what was it about me that made me know I could be a success.

I spoke from my heart. I said that even though I was only eighteen-years-old and I had never owned a business before, I knew that this is my destiny. I told him how much it meant to me. I told him all the work that I had done to prepare for this. I told him I was hard worker and that it was my dream. I told him I knew I could build a store that would bring the community together. A store with heart. A week later I received a call from the bank letting me know that I was approved. I knew in my heart this was what I truly wanted and apparently it showed.

How do you know what *you* really want? Your heart knows. Let it be your guide, and it will take you where you need to go if you listen to it.

Are you ready to impact the world with your unique voice?

Do you have a big, bold dream for your life?

Do you find yourself imagining the day you can turn your passion into a successful business?

Do you strive to do something heart-centered?

Does your heart speak to you when you ask yourself these questions? Keep listening.

You might not get an immediate answer. Instead look for whispers and subtle hints. Listen to them.

I really didn't know what this meant until last year shortly after my departure from my beverage company, which as you know, was a huge transition for me. In the middle of me "figuring" out my next step, one of my very close friends Jeanette surprised me with a trip to Arizona and tickets to a personal growth conference for my birthday.

I wasn't quite sure what the conference was about, but I was so grateful that she wanted me to go with her. A couple of days prior to the event, I was trying to research more about it, but couldn't find a listing of all the speakers. I mentioned it to her, and she hesitantly shared that at these types of conferences they don't tell you who the speakers are.

I was thinking, *what kind of conference doesn't tell you who the speakers are? Maybe a conference on Nigerian prince scams or a secret cult?* When I asked her further about it, she then added that it went from 8 a.m. to 7 p.m. each day. Then I thought, *what did I get myself into? Who can sit in a room for almost eleven hours?* I told her that I most likely wouldn't see all the speakers and that I would probably just listen to a few and then go enjoy the resort since it was sunny and 80 degrees. She then informed me, with even more hesitation that they actually like you to stay for the entire time. Then, I really thought *where are we going? What is this? A surprise trip to the dentist, or a destination wedding, or a destination dentist wedding?*

As is turned out, it was a life-changing experience. While I thought that I would want to hear one or two speakers and then go relax at the pool with a margarita, I actually didn't want to leave and miss hearing any of the speakers. So much so that even when I had to go to the bathroom I literally sprinted there and back in hopes that I wouldn't miss one morsel of inspiration. Then something serendipitous happened. The first day they announced an author of the book I'd just finished reading and loved, Rachel Hollis was going to be a speaker. I was thrilled to learn a woman was being represented in the midst of an all-male line-up. And she did not disappoint. She is the epitome of heart and hustle and she inspires me. I love that her speaking approach was unique from the male speakers. Don't get me wrong, the male speakers were inspirational, but she spoke directly to the audience. Down off the stage face to face, heart to heart. Something unexpectedly hit me when I saw her connect with the women in the audience and it was powerful. It was a revelation.

Being at the event opened my eyes. It opened my heart. I saw things in a way that I never thought I would see them. I realized that the business that I had been building for the past decade, the business that I wanted to incorporate so much heart into, the business that would ultimately inspire other people to follow their passion and dreams wouldn't have gotten me to where I ultimately wanted to go because it lost its heart.

I realized that this was now my opportunity to take everything I learned and create the purpose driven business I dreamed of. Listening to speaker after speaker, I became more encouraged that this was the path I was meant to be on. The more I connected with women at the conference and told my story, the more I could see how what I had to offer could potentially change lives. And people at the conference were telling me this right to my face. Over and over. I was overcome with emotion. The realization that I wanted to help inspire others became clearer as each hour went by.

I experienced an overwhelming feeling of gratitude for the opportunity to be there and see this incredible light. I knew then that this was my destiny. I will be forever grateful to Jeanette for such a special gift. It was my time to share my insight with the world from my heart.

If your heart speaks to you to create or do something new, it might feel scary. And depending on what messages you heard growing up, it can feel wrong to break away from tradition. Some people in your life may only feel comfortable with the conventional way of doing things. But that's okay. You are not them. Do not feel selfish for listening to what your heart wants. Embrace it.

I love this quote from Marie Forleo: "Living for other people's expectations guarantees you'll fall short of your own."

Don't let other people's expectations or influences mask your true self or mute our what your heart is telling you.

Despite all the outside influences and the ideas of what you "should" be doing, try bringing your heart into the equation. It will tell you what you need to hear.

My heart told me when I was in college that I wanted to be an entrepreneur and I didn't want to wait. I hustled and bought a franchise. The store opened with huge success and we became an integral part of the community. Our customers loved coming to the store.

I can remember vividly standing outside the store in the busy strip mall parking lot, looking up at the big store sign and thinking, *wow, this is really mine. I did it.* This was my store and I was nineteen-years-old. Within the first year we became the top grossing revenue store out of all the stores in the franchise. While we were successful, I made a lot of mistakes along the way, but they were all lessons learned that would be part of my toolkit in future businesses.

Heart is what drives us. It's believing in your success despite your naysayers and "Negative Nancys." It's about building positive, respectful relationships. It's about being true to who you are, your core values. It's about knowing when obstacles arise you will get through them. Being positive. Finding things to be grateful for and even laughing through the tough times. Working together as a team, supporting one another. Coming through for each other. In my beverage business it seemed like every week we were facing a new obstacle. Instead of going to the negative, I would always say, "You just have to laugh!" My employees always would tell me how much it meant to them that I would remain so positive in the face of those never-ending challenges.

Words can't really express how my dedicated team made me strive to do better and be better. I wanted to be the best leader and they gave me the opportunity to do that—with heart. I am extremely grateful to have had a such an outstanding team that allowed me to work hard and create a heart-centric company culture. The more I grew the company, the more I knew I wanted to impact people's lives.

Thomas John Watson, Sr. says it best: "To be successful, you have to have your heart in your business and your business in in your heart."

Hustling is important to accomplish our dreams, but heart is what we need *now*. I hustled like no one's business for my beverage brand to be successful but pouring my heart and soul in it made all the difference.

The heart of a business can take it from average to A+.

Sometimes it takes time to find what sets your heart on fire. It may be that you will love something you're talented at or you may develop a talent for something you love.

If we truly pay attention and take time to listen to our heart, we will hear it speaking. Nurture it and it will grow.

As a result of recently listening to my heart, I am now forging ahead with my "next chapter" helping women who are struggling with some of the challenges I have faced. To share my gift and my stories from my heart, authentically feeds my passion and purpose.

Having faith in what your heart is telling you takes courage but know that the heart is what fulfills us and gives our lives meaning. It's with heart that we impact others, emotionally evolve, and help the world around us with intention and love. Where would we be without that?

Love what you do and do what you love. Follow your heart, hustle, and happiness will follow.

This is the key to happiness.

My hope for you is that you'll wake up every day filled with excitement and ready to hustle like your life depends on it. Doing something you love that fills your heart with joy, and feeds others.

It's totally possible to do business in a positive, thoughtful way. And to make a meaningful impact, you have to step into your power fully and hustle. You have to own it.

Enter...the "Next Chapter"...literally, like the next chapter. Stay tuned!!

A few of my favorite tips to help you hustle with heart...

1. Get inspired! Learning from those who came before us is so critical. Listen to podcasts, speakers, and authors who touch your heart and inspire you. TED Talks are always a great go-to for inspiration. I love Cheryl Sandberg and Brené Brown. I also look for companies that are successful and have impactful mission statements. Companies who are growing and are also giving back. Read their stories. Learning about what or how they are doing it, inspires me with ideas. Look at companies like Tom's, Kimpton Hotels ("my home away from home" and my favorite hotel by far), Third Love, and Warby Parker.

2. If you could spend the rest of your life doing or talking about one thing, what would it be? Take some time to think about this one. Perhaps you love cooking and entertaining and want to share your recipes and party ideas with the world. Or maybe you love children and want to set up a foundation to raise awareness nationally for special needs. Once something comes to mind, just start writing. You might be surprised what you discover.

3. What makes you feel alive? What lights you up? Think from the heart and write it down. It could be things like:

- Running a marathon
- Throwing a dinner party
- Spending time with your children
- Traveling the world

Once you have your list, what are the things you can incorporate into your life or business?

> Glow Girl Affirmation:
> I can be kind, fierce, and brave—
> all at the same time.

14

Next Chapter

"For what it's worth: It's never too late to be whoever you want to be. I hope you live a life you're proud of, and if you find that you're not, I hope you have the strength to start over."

—*F. Scott Fitzgerald*

THIS LAST CHAPTER is your next chapter. This is not the end, it's just the beginning. Today is the first day of the rest of your life and you are fully prepared to write your own story, sister! Not just any story, but a "bestseller!"

What can be more perfect than a new beginning?

In order to invent the life you want you have to be willing to let go of what's not working or what's holding you back. Your story doesn't end here because of a few rough chapters. Take it from me!

When you let go of what didn't work or the bad experiences you endured, you create room to find your passion and feel inspired again.

Love your past. It's not what happened to you that determines your outcome, it's how you handle what's happened to you.

Life is tough, but sister, so are you.

Your life might have been messy and bumpy. It might have

been riddled with mistakes, anxiety, and fear. But all those things were catalysts to help you become a better, wiser, and more courageous version of yourself. So, embrace your story and how much you've grown from it. Be proud of what you've done and for wanting to create a better life for yourself.

You can't start the next chapter of your life if you keep re-reading the last one.

Love this quote from Maria Shriver: "At some point, all of us will experience a resurrection in our lives. We'll get knocked down, have to rewrite our narrative, and have to rise up and make that new story work for us."

Rise up, sister!

You can rise up from misfortune, trauma, or despair. But you have to decide. Only you. You have to decide to not let it push you down and take your power away. You have to decide that this is just a page or a chapter in your life and *you* have the ability to write a spectacular life-changing "bestseller."

These pages are all part of your story and make you who you are. And who you are is destined for greatness.

We are only *one* decision away from a totally different life.

So now is your time. What kind of story are you going to write?

Do you want to start a business? Is there something you're truly passionate about? What is your unrealized dream?

Knowing your strengths, talents, and abilities is the first step to unleashing your potential and power and creating meaning and lasting transformation. We are all blessed with so many wonderful gifts, but we can't unwrap and share them with others if we fail to acknowledge what they are. It's time to acknowledge your gifts!

Go back to when you were a child. What did you like to do? As you got older what have you held on to? What experiences have you gone through, and what have you learned from them? What talents do people compliment you on? If money was no object, what would you want to spend your time doing?

Ask yourself these questions. Don't over think them. Do you notice a theme? There could be more than one, but you can sometimes find a way to combine two or three passions into one cool idea or purpose. For example, you love food and travel. You could create a food inspired travel blog or a food tour company in popular travel destinations.

If a passion from your childhood resonates with you, think of something you could do or create as an adult. Like if you loved ballet, maybe you could open a dance studio, maybe you could teach dance to underprivileged children, or maybe you could create a fun dance workout class that becomes a nationwide movement!

As Elizabeth Gilbert says, "Do whatever brings you to life, then. Follow your own fascinations, obsessions, and compulsions. Trust them. Create whatever causes a revolution in your heart."

You can do anything you set your mind to with some research, lots of hard work and never-ending persistence. Regardless of how old you are, what tools or resources you have, you have a gift and it's your job to find a way to share it with the world. The purpose of life is to discover your gift. The meaning of life is to give that gift away, but you must know what you have first.

The key to living your best life is to live your purpose.

Maybe you had dreams you put on the back-burner to raise your children or care for a family member. Or you had to hold on to your job because it provided stability for your family.

Well, sister, now it's your time to shine! You can do this.

At any given moment you have the power to say, *this is not how my story is going to end.*

We all have self-doubts and if everyone listened to them,

there wouldn't be all the brilliant entrepreneurs that exist today. Imagine if Bill Gates said to himself, *creating an operating system is not practical or realistic so why bother?* Where would technology be today if he didn't follow his passion with confidence?

What if *you* are the one that's meant to change people's lives?

Limitations are only in your mind. There are too many successful people out there who prove exactly that. If you believe there are limitations, then there are.

Are you allowing yourself to consider what you are possible of?

Could I have easily said, *I don't know anything about the beverage industry so how can I possibly create a beverage brand that could be sold in stores like Target and major grocery chains?* Hell yes! I never worked for a beverage company, I wasn't a flavor chemist, I had never even seen a beverage manufacturing plant. I also didn't have contacts to retail stores or restaurants, and I didn't know how or where to go to create a formula to get my product bottled. But did I let any of those obstacles stop me? Hell no! Why? Because this was my passion. I wanted to build an all-natural organic delicious tasting beverage to make people happy. And once it became a success, I could then take the story of my journey and help inspire others to follow their passion.

To succeed you must believe in something with such a passion that it becomes a reality.

Were there times along my journey where I thought to myself, *why am I doing this? Who's going to buy my beverage?* Were there nights that I would cry myself to sleep because I didn't know how I was going to get money to pay for the next production run or payroll? Absolutely! But I didn't let it stop me. For every "no" there is a "yes" and I believed I would find the solution.

Don't look at the people who haven't made it, look at the

people who have. Look at the successful entrepreneurs and follow what they did. Research it. Memorize it. Live it.

You become what you believe.

If you want this bad enough you will give it your all and that will be the difference between the entrepreneur that's successful and the one that doesn't get to see what they could have accomplished.

Are you willing to suspend fear and move forward ruthlessly toward your goals?

When I was building the Sipp brand, I worked through the night and typically slept on average two to three hours a night. I knew I needed to make this sacrifice to get the brand off the ground. But it was my choice and I wanted to do it. I was driven to do it. I was too excited to sleep. There were so many people I needed to tell about my new organic beverage.

I researched celebrities who were making the change to organic. I saw that Tori Spelling tweeted quite a bit about her organic garden. One night at about 2:30 a.m. I decided to tweet about my beverage to let her know about it. I was dreaming big, but these are the chances I took. About ten minutes after my tweet suggesting she should try Sipp, she connected with me and we were messaging each other! She became a Sipp fan and was kind enough to provide a quote for my website!

This shows us that if we think small and say things like, *why bother, she gets contacted by hundreds of people*, we might be missing out on life-changing opportunities.

Are you ready to work toward your dream life regardless of obstacles or what others say or think?

Pursue your passion and when you meet obstacles it will give you the fuel to keep going. Use the tools to combat your Negative Nancy. And never let someone tell you can't do something because it sounds crazy or it's never been done. Don't let them stop you from chasing you dream.

Have the courage to be yourself and don't try to fit into someone else's vision of what they think your life should look like. Don't reach for someone else's life, reach for yours. You may need to give some things up from the past to move on. Old habits, negative people, clutter. But trust me, you will gain something in return when you do. Letting go of any toxicity from the past will only lighten your baggage on your journey moving forward.

Ask yourself, do the people in your tribe support the life you're trying to create?

What are the things you need to let go of?

Let go of the people holding you back. There are too many people who are grateful for who you are for you to obsess over the few that don't. Let them go and forge forward.

What's the gift you have that can be shared with the world? What's the song only you can sing?

Don't limit your dreams. Dream big. No one else can do what you do and how you do it.

Trust yourself and have the faith. We all have an inner compass, but it can lose direction when we don't listen. When we ignore it because it may be directing us to do something that many people around us aren't doing. Then maybe that means you're supposed to do exactly that thing. Maybe you're supposed to be the one.

Don't be afraid of yourself. Don't play small.

After building the Sipp brand, I thought I should create another beverage company because that's what I know and everyone around me agreed. It's what I had done for the past ten years so it just made sense.

However, when the passion is strong enough, you will act in spite of what seems logical. I felt this when I began writing this book. One day while I was writing for hours, self-doubt temporarily took over and I thought, *why am I dedicating all my time to this book when I don't even know if anyone will read it?* I told myself I should be working on a new beverage brand or doing more consulting with beverage companies. I stopped typing and I felt a wave come over me, something I never felt before. My face felt flush and suddenly tears were uncontrollably streaming down my face. This was a feeling I can't even explain. I mean, trust me, I can cry fairly easily, but this was coming from someplace deep down. I knew I had to keep going. This was something beyond my control. Something much deeper than a little book I wanted to write and share. This was my purpose.

I believed I could help women. I believed I could change women's lives.

Who are you without limitations?

I want you to think about that for moment. Do you doubt yourself when you think of your passion or purpose? Do you feel you might not be the best? Do you feel like it's too late to try now?

Only when you dare to do the very thing you doubt you can do; will you realize how little you ever needed to doubt yourself to begin with.

And just because you haven't achieved your dreams by now doesn't mean it's too late. Fulfilling a lifelong passion at forty or beyond I think is more magical than at twenty-five. So much more has happened to you in those forty years that could hold you back, so when you achieve your dreams later in life, it's pretty spectacular.

Dreams don't have an expiration date. It's never too late to share your gift.

Think about this, would you rather live with failure or regret? Failure means you tried, and regret means you'll never know. Don't wait around for something to fall in your lap or for someone to give you their permission or approval to do something great.

You don't ever want to feel like you could have, should have, or would have.

Don't worry about inconveniencing someone or how it will affect your children. Show them who you are. Show them how you follow your passion and pursue your dreams. Be a strong powerful role-model. #glowyourownway

Is someone or something holding you back from doing what you truly want to do?

Your growth may scare people who don't want to change. Some people will love you as long as you fit in *their* box. Don't be with people who validate your excuses or help you stay stuck in a box. Remove yourself from situations and people who can't, or refuse, to accept you as you are or are striving to become.

Refuse to live silently in somebody else's idea of who you should be.

As a child, I had a pretty big imagination. Whether I was carving sculptures from wood I found and selling them in our driveway for a quarter, writing plays, creating cabaret like skits with my cousin, or pretending to be Harriet the Spy and going on an adventure of discovery on foot that unexpectedly took me miles from my home, I was always creating. I was always going toward freedom and independence. I had my own ideas, desires, and values. Becoming an entrepreneur was the only way I could achieve what motivated me.

I created a successful beverage brand and it gave me everything I wanted. But I had an eye-opening epiphany just before writing this book. My confidence was fueled by Sipp. People loved Sipp and Sipp was *my* creation. I was proud of my brand so then I was proud of myself. I realized I hid behind my beverage brand.

So now without my beverage brand, who was I? My company was my purpose for ten years and now what? What did I have to offer now? What was my purpose?

What you love to do is your purpose.

Truthfully, it was a rough transition and even as I told myself that Sipp was a stepping stone to my next big venture, I don't know that I truly believed that 100%. When the self-doubt kicked in, I thought that maybe Sipp was my last big hurrah. Maybe there wasn't anything left in me. I already had successful businesses in the past. Maybe this was my final chapter.

Don't look at your detours as denials. It might just mean it's leading you to something better.

The truth is, sister, things are going to happen to us, and we will continue to be given challenges. There will always be problems, but we need to focus on what's great and positive. Don't let your problems define you—let them sculpt you. I realized that Sipp was not my final chapter. I'm now stronger and more resilient because of what I persevered through. Problems make us become more. And don't we want to be more?

Strong women don't play victim. They don't blame. They put their big girl panties on and deal!

So far, you've survived everything you thought you wouldn't.

The reality is that we all wanted that *Leave it to Beaver* picture perfect family, but what family is perfect? We should embrace the imperfections of our family just like we do with ourselves. Instead of blaming our parents for everything they did to us, we should be grateful. You wouldn't be here right now fighting to learn and grow to be the best version of yourself, working so hard to rise to your greatness.

Stars can't shine without darkness.

So, while at times things were not easy for me in the past, if I had those "ideal" parents, I would not be the woman I am proud to be today. My childhood experiences were an invitation to take the journey into myself, to love myself, heal myself, and ultimately find my gift to help to transform others.

I love this quote from C.S. Lewis: "You can't go back and

change the beginning, but you can start where you are and change the ending."

I realize it may be difficult to dream of a life you've never seen or that was never modeled for you. The life you dream of may see so far out of reach to you. How you were raised and what you were taught to believe may have sent you messages like you can't dream big or why bother, you'll only be disappointed. But these thoughts you've come to believe are not truly *you*, they were instilled in you.

Once you realize that naturally you can do anything and that *you* hold the key to your big bright future, you can begin to create the life you desire.

So, my question to you now is, do you know what you want to achieve? Maybe you want to build a business, land your dream job, or learn to be happier with the life you have.

Every day is a chance to become a better version of yourself. Not to say you aren't great already, but there's always room for growth and improvement. I firmly believe that in life we can never stop learning, we can never stop growing and we can always find ways to better ourselves. In order to do that, it all starts in how we think. Everything is all about perspective and your mindset. Focus on the positive and change your thoughts. This can change your overall sense of being and way of life.

Make something small happen every day. One step at a time. Faster is not always better and you don't need to hit it out of the ballpark. I know it's hard work following a dream but it's about perseverance and patience. And if it's your dream, it's so worth it!

Nobody gets successful or rich overnight. It may look that way when you look at social media, but I guarantee there was struggle behind that story. Don't compare someone else's end to your middle. Know you're on the right path, believe in yourself, keep hustling, and celebrate every milestone along the way!

Reaching any of your goals big or small are all wins.

Celebrating these wins will remind you of your ability, hard work, and give you the drive to continue on with your purpose. I always made a point to celebrate *every* win. Whether it was a nice dinner out, a bottle of champagne, or a meaningful token to remember that special moment.

One of my most meaningful "gifts" was when I received funding for my business. A few weeks before, I was eating lunch in a café and saw a woman with a red shiny Coach purse. Honestly, I don't even really like the color red (or the word "red") but it caught my eye and it looked like a "power" bag. After lunch, I walked to the Coach store down the street. There it was. On the shelf in all its glory. I picked it up and I knew this was going to be mine. I told myself (and my journal) that if I received the investment, I was going to celebrate by rewarding myself with this bag. I got the funding and I got the bag! (Side note, I bought it on eBay at a discount! #bargainhustle)

It takes a lot of work to get to where you deserve to go, but you can do this. Embrace the tools I provide in this book and use them. Use them every day. Use them until they become a habit and you will see changes begin to happen. You'll feel the transformation. Just imagine what that will feel like? I'm here to tell you what an incredible feeling it is to move beyond the shame, limiting beliefs, and all the damage that we have done to ourselves.

The life you wish you could be living is waiting for you to begin living it. Go get it!

Believe that your presence makes a positive impact in the world. If you are unsure about whether you have anything of value to bring to the table, you can dispel any such doubt simply by showing up. Share your own unique energy of positivity and watch it spread. Share your gift. Being true to your authentic enthusiasm is fuel to help turn any ship in a promising direction.

What if God put something on your heart for a reason? I

had no idea I had a book in me until I felt it in my heart, and I knew I had to do it. If we all lived life in pursuit of what we were meant to do, imagine how magnificent the world would be.

Someone said this to me once and it changed me forever: "You have a gift and if you don't share it, you're doing people a disservice."

I am living my purpose and I love every minute of the work I do now. Consulting, mentoring, and writing. Most of all inspiring. I thought that my beverage company was everything I ever worked for and dreamed of. I met and surpassed my goals in my business. But little did I know there was so much more ahead of me. My beverage company was actually only part of my journey and a stepping stone on the path to my next adventure, sharing my gifts with others.

If you serve the world, the world will serve you.

Writing this book has been an emotional roller coaster ride filled with joy, excitement, fear laughter, and many tears. It is been such a transformational journey. It unexpectedly changed my life. Through my desire to share my stories to empower you, I also empowered myself. I am woman and hear me roar! I am on fire and I am glowing for all to see and I want that for you!

Todd said this to me when I was in the midst of writing this book and I saw myself transforming, *the best way to learn is to teach*. It's so true. I know now I have a voice and a message to share that's deeply needed.

Years ago, if someone told me that I would be writing a book about my life and my experiences to share with other women and hopes to inspire them to live their best lives, I would've never believed it. I couldn't imagine sharing my life with the world. I tell you this because it's so important to let you know the mindset I was in to where I am now; writing this book and feeling so honored to share my story with you.

"When we deny our stories, they define us. When we own our stories, we get to write the ending." I posted this quote from Brené Brown on social media a year ago and here I am now sharing my story.

The key to finding purpose in our life is to honor all that we are right at this moment and all we have been through. It's about owning our stories along with all the wisdom they have taught us. It's about knowing every experience was essential to shape our character into the person we are today and valuing ourselves.

The choices I've made give my entire life meaning, good or bad. You know by now that this didn't come easy for me. This life-changing journey that brought me to where I am now and will continue to carry me forward, was filled with many dark times where I didn't know if I could rise above.

We rise by lifting others.

What I truly desire for each and every one of you is to know how amazingly spectacular you are and know that you are reading this book because you want so much more in your life and somewhere deep down inside you know that you deserve it. And I'm here to tell you that you absolutely do.

Being yourself is a precious gift that only you can give the world. So, without caring what other people think, start telling your story. Embrace all of you. Be your authentic self. When you strip away all those labels and just let go you are allowing your real self to shine!

I love this quote: "The strongest actions for a woman is to love herself, be herself, and shine amongst those who never believed she could."

I believe in my heart that the greatness inside you and the life you want to live is possible. I know this is because I made it possible for myself. Whatever it is your heart desires—I hope to be your shining beacon of light. I believe in you.

I heard a story a while back and it's about a glow stick.

Most of you know what a glow stick is; colorful neon rods of light, but it doesn't glow by itself until you break it. Just like a glow stick we were created to glow. If we stand still and don't move, we are not doing what we were created to do. Once a glow stick is broken it starts to glow. It's fulfilling its purpose.

I've faced many challenges and hardships over the years. My dad's battle with cancer, my marriage, my business—and there were times I broke down. When I was broken it was bad. But I had to get up and keep going and with a lot of work I now clearly see what my purpose is. Without those trials and tribulations how would I know? How can you see the good when you don't know the bad? We were all created to glow and sometimes we need to break before we can shine.

Be willing to show yourself; fully claim all that you are and all that you've survived.

If you hold back, it will keep you from accomplishing the greatness you are capable of and living the life you deserve. Step out of the shadows and shine!

Show your glow and make the world a brighter place. #showyourglow

It's your time now to rise. It's your time now to stand up for yourself. It's your time now to use your voice. You've got this and I am so beyond excited to see where you "glow." I'm so eager to see how you will move along on your journey and the life-changing stories you will be sharing.

Make space for the next version of you because she's coming and she's pretty damn amazing!

Push past the walls of your comfort zone and break free from the self-doubt and limiting beliefs that have kept you trapped from rising to your best life. Be bold, be brave, and shine bright.

The light that glows inside us connects us to each other and everything else in the world. The brighter your light shines the more you will be leading the path for other women to go on their spectacular journey. Just imagine as one of us starts down the path shining brightly, the more women will continue, one after the other, until we are this enormous glowing body of light and no one will be able to blow it out. #glowtogether

The world needs your light to shine!

My final wish is that just one person reads my book and decides not to give up. Realize how blessed you are. You have the power to create the life you desire.

This quote from J.M. Barrie holds so much meaning for me: "The moment you doubt whether you can fly, you cease forever to be able to do it…to have faith is to have wings."

I'm still building those wings, but just in different ways now and they are always new and improved taking me higher and higher. I know it's not easy but don't let the fear of falling keep you from flying! When a bird is sitting on a tree, she's not afraid of the branch breaking because her trust isn't in the branch, it's in her wings. Always believe in yourself and fly high!

Be the light you were born to be. Now is your time to shine!

Never forget, *you* write your own story. Make it one you will never forget.

You glow, girl!

A few of my favorite favorite tips to help you create your "next chapter"…

The secret to having it all is believing you already do. Start living like you already possess the change you want.

1. Vision to Glow: Are you ready to "glow?"

   I realize change can be scary and challenging. When we try to force finding our true purpose it can be overwhelming. You may not know where to begin or you may have so many passions you don't know which one to choose or start with. This may make you feel discouraged and defeated before you even start.

Here is one of many things I learned in therapy: It's about the journey, not about the destination.

Take one step at a time. It's good to plan but you don't need to have *everything* figured out right now. You can plan your steps to make progress to where you want to go.

So instead of creating your entire bestseller all at once, just go page by page or chapter by chapter. Then you can take small doable steps towards creating your masterpiece.

They key is your imagination. That's how we discover our deepest desires. By going deeper, and understanding yourself better, you create a better balance. By gaining clarity through visualization, you can see yourself moving through the fear or challenges so that you can fully begin to embrace your passions and rising to your best life in alignment with your purpose.

So, let's begin doing our Vision to Glow by reading the questions below. I recommend someone read them to you so you can fully concentrate with your eyes closed, but if you don't have someone to read them, then close your eyes after each set of questions. Try not to answer the questions verbally. Use your imagination to visualize. Essentially "see" the answers.

Have your journal or something you can takes notes with close by.

Get into a comfortable position and close your eyes.

Begin with imagining your perfect day. A day that's so incredibly perfect you could live it over and over. Now imagine living this day one year from now. This is your ideal day.

Imagine exactly what you want, with all the details, and feel like you already have it.

Where are you living? What's it like around you? What do you see? How do you feel? Who are you with, if anyone? What's your morning routine like? Do you work out? When do you start your workday? Where are you working? What does it look like? Who do you work with? How do you feel doing this work? Do you feel fulfilled?

Do you stop working for lunch? Where do you eat? Who are you with? What type of lunch are you eating? How are you feeling?

How do you finish out your day? Do you work out now? Do you meet up with friends? Who are your friends? Do you feel like you accomplished a lot?

Where do you eat dinner? Do you cook? How are you feeling? What time do you go to bed? What is your evening routine? How do you feel thinking about this ideal day before you go to sleep? What words describe your day?

When you feel you're ready, open your eyes and write down everything you saw and how you felt. Now think of one action you can take to move your dream towards a reality.

2. Journaling dreams (goals) and gratitude: This has been life changing for me. Journal three things you're grateful for, big or small. Gratitude work is so important to improve self-esteem. When you take the time to focus on the good things in your life you naturally become more positive.

Journal ten dreams you want to happen. Keeping your dreams and goals at the top of your mind is key. Set very specific goals and don't play small, dream big.

These are your dreams and you can make them as big as you would like!

3. Vision Board: A vision board is usually designed with big poster board that has a collage of different pictures of wants and dreams you wish to fulfill. This is a way to further manifest you Vision to Glow. What images did you see during your visualization? Find these images in magazines or print them out online and attached them to a board that you can place in a room that you frequent. The key is to see these images every day as if you are already living it. The brain works in symbols and images. When you can find images that depict what you want or where you want to go, your subconscious is going to work to get you there.

Glow Girl Affirmation:
I believe in the person I am becoming.

Acknowledgements

To EVERYONE WHO inspired me to write this book and for all your support and encouragement along the way, I thank you from the bottom of my heart. So many people have impacted me on the journey of my life, I would need pages and pages to acknowledge everyone!

Thank you to my son, Devin, who is always by my side through all my endeavors, believing in me, challenging me, supporting me when I doubt myself, understanding how much time it takes to build something you dream of, for accepting me for who I am. I hope I'm showing you what courage and perseverance looks like and how important it is to share your gifts with the world. And for all the times you said, "just finish the book!" Guess what? I finished it! Love you.

Thank you to my parents for being there for me and for all you've done. And for the parts of you who made me who I am today. The creativity, compassion, inventiveness, drive, resilience and stubbornness. Mom, thank you for supporting me and encouraging me on this journey. I love you, Dad; I know you are up there cheering me on. You are always in my heart.

To Todd, my beacon of light and hope. Thank you for showing me I can do anything, despite all my limiting beliefs and self-doubts that you helped to break down. You taught me what thoughts were irrational and how to cope with challenges. You showed me different perspectives that I couldn't see. You taught me that my past doesn't define my future. You believed in me when I didn't believe in myself. You gave me courage to share my story with the world and most importantly, you taught me that everything I ever needed, I already had inside of myself. You changed my life and I will be forever grateful.

Donna, you are the angel who unexpectedly entered my life and selflessly gave of yourself. You not only gave me a beautiful gift, but also my dad, in the last year of his life. You were his ray of sunshine in the midst of his darkness. Your strength and support carried me through one of the most difficult, scariest, and heartbreaking times of my life. I will be forever grateful, sister.

To my longtime supportive friend, Jeanette, who gave me the gift of a life-changing personal growth experience that sparked the flame inside me and opened the possibilities for me to share my stories with the world. Thank you for always encouraging me, supporting me, and reminding me how far I've come and what great things I still can accomplish.

To Carly, Emily, Kelly, and Matt—my spectacular Sipp employees who became my family. Thank you for always going above and beyond for me. Thank you for having my back and doing whatever needed to be done to help me build my business. I couldn't have done it without you. I am so blessed you all came into my life and are now supporting me on my new journey. We will always be family and I'm so grateful. A special thanks to Kelly for your creative photography skills and knowing what I really wanted for my book cover design.

Heather, you've been by my side through it all. You believed in me and supported me, when at times I didn't believe in myself. We have such a special bond. Our "sister" trips will always hold a special place in my heart, and I can't wait for the many more to come!

To Shalini, you brighten my world on dark days. You listened to my story, even when I was afraid to share. You were there for me through the rough times and together we created light. Lots of light and laughter (and dance)! And to Sharon, our special "sister weekend" memories with the three of us always bring me so much joy.

To Emme and Melissa, my "dream team!" So blessed you both came in my life and together we are stronger. Women power! I love how we all lift each other when we are down, encourage each other to keep persevering, and how we always see the gifts we have in each other. You are my glow-getters!

Mary, thank you for all your support, always. From the very beginning you believed in my crazy idea of an organic beverage brand and fast forward to now, you're here supporting me in my "next chapter." I'm so grateful to be your "daughter."

To my editor, Josh. I originally thought I would work with a female editor since I was writing a women's empowerment book, but once I read your sample I knew you were the one to edit my book. You understood where I was coming from, you pushed me at times to be more vulnerable, and you praised my writing and voice. You assured me that my message will help many women which encouraged me to forge forward. It's not easy to pour your heart and soul out for all the world to see, but I couldn't have asked for a better partner to be by my side through this process. I am truly blessed. Thank you.

To all my friends, family, Sipp colleagues, and supporters, thank you for being by my side. To my awesome bro friends and colleagues for *always* supporting me. Andrew T., Andrew C., Matt C., Jon, Eric, Domenick, John H., Kiran, John F., Ulysse, Bob M x 2, and Ron's crew—you are all part of my "story." Thank you to Maria, Nadja, Katrina, Cindy, Annette, Brenda, Nina and Gina. Thank you for encouraging me to write this book and continually reminding me I have an important story to share that will help women change their lives.

To all my readers—I am who I am because of all of you. I want to thank you for coming on this wonderful crazy journey with me and letting me in your heart. I'm so honored.

All of you inspire me to be the best I can be, and I hope you have found bits and pieces in my journey to help create your own roadmap to greatness, to rise your best life and shine!

Let's all glow together!

xo,

Beth

Made in the
USA
Middletown, DE